WAKE UP
OUR SOULS

WAKE UP
OUR SOULS

A Celebration of Black American Artists

Tonya Bolden

PUBLISHED IN ASSOCIATION WITH THE SMITHSONIAN AMERICAN ART MUSEUM

HARRY N. ABRAMS, INC.

ACKNOWLEDGMENTS

Everlasting gratitude to my editor, Howard W. Reeves, for his vision and for helping me see the forest when I spiraled into an obsession over trees. I also thank his assistant, Linas Alsenas, for his cheerful efficiency in an array of matters; and thanks as well to production editor Andrea Colvin, art director Becky Terhune, and designer Celina Carvalho for their help in making the book shine.

And then there's my collaborator: the Smithsonian American Art Museum. Special thanks to its director Betsy Broun, senior curator Virginia Mecklenburg, and editors Susan Efird, Tiffany Farrell, and Sara Beyer. Extra-special thanks to the museum's chief of publications, Theresa Slowik, for providing me with a wealth of research materials, and for sharing her knowledge and insights.

Lastly, I wish to thank the artists or their estates and the photographers who contributed their portraits.

Designer: Celina Carvalho

You may visit Tonya Bolden's Web site at www.tonyabolden.com

Library of Congress Cataloging-in-Publication Data
Bolden, Tonya.
Wake up our souls / by Tonya Bolden.
p. cm.
Summary: Presents a history of African American visual arts and artists from the days of slavery to the present.
Includes bibliographical references and index.
ISBN 0-8109-4527-4
1. African-American art—Juvenile literature. 2. African-American artists—Biography—Juvenile literature.
[1. African-American art. 2. Artists. 3. African-Americans—Biography.] I. Title.
N6538.N5B65 2004
704.03'96073—dc22
2003016972

Harry N. Abrams, Inc.
100 Fifth Avenue, New York, NY 10011
www.abramsbooks.com
Abrams is a subsidiary of
LA MARTINIÈRE
GROUPE

Smithsonian American Art Museum

CONTENTS

James A. Porter
(1905–1970)

Many artists use events and people from their own lives as subjects for their art. James Porter made numerous portraits of his family and friends and this still life remembers a place and a moment in his life. His wife, Dorothy Porter, fondly recalled the day in 1949 when she marched in a procession as the embodiment of "Alma Mater" at Howard University's May Festival. For the occasion, she carried a large bouquet of peonies. On their return home, her husband arranged the flowers near a stair landing, and began painting. In the resulting painting, *Still Life with Peonies*, the blossoms dominate the picture's space and repeat colors from the banister, the wall, and the canvas at the lower right. The rigid vertical lines of the striped wallpaper, the door casings, and the balusters are an effective contrast with

the flowers' exuberant freedom.

The versatile Porter was a painter, an art historian, and teacher, having taught for many years at Howard University. He published his main contribution to art scholarship, *Modern Negro Art*, in 1943. It was the first history of artists of African descent in America.

*STILL LIFE WITH
PEONIES*
1949
BY JAMES A. PORTER
OIL ON CANVAS
40 X 30 1/8 IN.

INTRODUCTION

From the beginning, people around the world have had an impulse—a need, some would say—to make visual their memories, pleasures, pains, hopes, and histories. We call both the process and the product "visual art."

Black Americans have made stellar contributions to the vast galaxy of visual art. How to decide which artists to include was not an easy task. But the desire to include a range of human experiences and mediums used was paramount. The stories of many artists are provided within the body of the book, but spotlights on others give fuller context to the discussion. To that effect, *Wake Up Our Souls* is not meant to be a comprehensive history of the black American artistic legacy or an analysis of the artists' techniques, but rather a look at the lives and creations of a small number of men and women who are part of a larger story—one that began several hundred years ago when the nation was new.

May you find in this mix, art that awakens, romances, or makes dance your soul, and enhances your appreciation of visual art.

NOTE TO READER: Alongside each artwork, there is a credit line containing the title of the work, year it was completed, name of the artist, medium used to create the work, and its dimensions.

Oak Trees (DETAIL)
1876
BY EDWARD MITCHELL BANNISTER
OIL ON CANVAS
33 7/8 X 60 1/4 IN.

EARLY
STRIVINGS

From austere or elaborate masks to wood and ivory carvings, from head-dresses to copper sculptures—people of present-day Angola, Benin, Congo, and other West African nations, have, for centuries, created an abundance of astounding works of art for various rites and rituals.

West Africa was the homeland for the majority of children and adults kidnapped for enslavement in America. Forced labor, beatings, and other horrors of captivity did not crush the soul-call to create, nor did they obliterate Africans' artistic abilities. African artistry survived, as evidenced by the patchwork quilts and intricately carved walking sticks the captives created. Other examples include *adinkra* symbols incorporated into ironwork such as that which graced Southern mansion gates and balconies, often made by enslaved blacksmiths.

In seventeenth- and eighteenth-century America, people were accustomed to blacks (enslaved and free) as artisans, as creators of objects used in everyday life or for decoration. But because the myth of black intellectual inferiority and emotional immaturity was widespread outside of black communities, most people did not take seriously the notion of a black person as an artist.

Joshua Johnson of Baltimore, Maryland, was among the first blacks in America to become a professional artist. Details of his life are few, and scholars have long debated his race, his birth and death dates, even the spelling of his name (Johnson or Johnston). If anyone ever captured his likeness, it has not survived. In recent years scholars have found a bill of sale and certificate of manumission recorded in the Baltimore County Courts in July 1782 for "the mulatto Joshua Johnson." George Johnson, a white man, acknowledged Joshua as his son and purchased him out of slavery from a farmer, William Wheeler Sr. The artist's mother was an unnamed slave, and the certificate stated that he would be freed when he completed his apprenticeship as a blacksmith or when he reached the age of twenty-one, whichever came first. Johnson was "upwards of nineteen years" in 1782, and was first listed as a portrait painter in Baltimore directories in 1796. There is no doubt that in freedom Johnson supported his family in part or in whole as a portraitist, from about 1795 until

PAGES FROM BALTIMORE COUNTY COURT RECORDS SHOW THE BILL OF SALE AND CERTIFICATE OF MANUMISSION THAT FREED JOSHUA JOHNSON (BORN CA. 1763, ACTIVE 1790–1825) FROM SLAVERY.

PORTRAIT OF ADELIA ELLENDER
ABOUT 1830–1832
BY JOSHUA JOHNSON
OIL ON CANVAS
26 1/4 X 21 1/8 IN.

Joshua Johnson surrounded this child with symbols of life's fragility. Both the flowers and the moth will fade within a week, while the cherries will ripen early in summer and then be gone. But a careful if slightly superstitious mother has put coral beads around her daughter's neck, which were once thought to ward off such childhood ills as colic, blood disorders, and whooping cough. This child's family lived at a time when many children died before reaching the age of eight. Her parents were conscious of this fact when they hired Johnson to make a record of her appearance at such an early age. Johnson prided himself on his skill and accuracy; the child's direct gaze is charming, and the lace and frills of the dress are delicately painted. The reds in the beads, shoes, and background unify the composition.

about 1825. And the best record we have of his life is his work.

Johnson was confident in his skills and constantly seeking new business. In the late 1790s he ran an ad in a Baltimore newspaper, the *Intelligencer,* in which he presented himself as a "self-taught genius" who had "experienced many insuperable obstacles in the pursuit of his studies." He assured potential customers of his "ability to execute all commands, with an effect, and in a style, which must give satisfaction." His customers must have been happy with his work, because he remained in business long enough to complete at least eighty surviving works, and by 1824 he was wealthy enough to buy parcels of land in three Maryland counties. All of his known subjects but two were white.

Like Joshua Johnson, women in early America who wanted to be professional artists faced obstacles. At the time, and long into the future, most people would believe that a woman should not seek a profession. While social pressure made many women abandon their hopes of being artists, some, like Edmonia Lewis, held fast to their dreams.

Unlike Johnson, Lewis was a Northerner who never knew slavery; this did not mean she had an easy life. By the time she was about nine years old, both her father, who was black, and her mother, who was part black and part Ojibwa (also known as Chippewa), had died. Though orphaned, little Edmonia was not without family: two maternal aunts took her in and raised her in a community near Niagara Falls.

Lewis also had an older brother, Samuel (she would later call him Sunrise). He made sure Edmonia received an excellent education. Having prospered in California during the gold rush (1848–1864), Samuel could afford to send her to one of the first American colleges to admit women and people of color: Oberlin College, in Oberlin, Ohio, an antislavery stronghold.

EDMONIA LEWIS
(1843/1845–AFTER 1911)

In the fall of 1859, fourteen-year-old Lewis entered Oberlin's high school. Even as she studied a variety of subjects—composition, botany, algebra, and the Bible, among them—Lewis kept up with the whirlwind of events as America hurtled toward the Civil War (1861–1865). One of the most dramatic was John Brown's famous raid.

On a mid-October night in 1859, the strident, white abolitionist John Brown led a small band of men on a raid of a United States armory and arsenal at Harpers Ferry, Virginia (now part of West Virginia). Brown's goal was to provide the spark that would ignite an all-out war against slaveholders and wipe away the stain of slavery. Brown's scheme failed miserably. Many of his raiders were shot dead soon after they attacked the armory. Others, like Brown, were eventually captured, tried for treason, convicted, then hanged. Osborne Anderson was the only raider to elude capture.

Many at Oberlin had known two of Brown's other black companions. John Copeland was a former student, and his uncle, Lewis Leary, was co-owner of a harness-making business in town. On Christmas Day, a memorial service was held for Leary and Copeland and, along with many townspeople, college faculty, and students, Lewis attended. The image of these men as martyrs was burned into her mind.

Within a few years, Edmonia would endure suffering herself. Two white students accused her of slipping something poisonous into their beverages. Lewis swore she was innocent, but many did not believe her. Worse, some decided to take the law into their own hands: On a February night in 1862, shortly before her hearing, a gang of vigilantes snatched Edmonia and took her to a field. There they beat her and left her unconscious in the snow, presumably to die.

Not only did Lewis live, she was eventually acquitted of the charges; however, her presence at Oberlin remained a point of controversy. In the end, the school dealt with the problem by refusing to allow her to register for her final term.

Moses (after Michelangelo)
1875
by Edmonia Lewis
marble
26 3/4 x 11 1/2 x 13 5/8 in.

Edmonia Lewis arrived in Italy in 1865 and completed this copy of Michelangelo's much larger *Moses* about a decade later. Nineteenth-century tourists often commissioned small copies of famous works as souvenirs. A commission such as this gave Lewis a chance to practice her skills and provided welcome income. She probably sold a number of these copies, which prove her sensitivity to the original and her mastery of the medium.

Lewis's ordeals at Oberlin left her with both physical and emotional scars. Despite this, or perhaps because of it, she devoted her life to creating beauty. While at Oberlin, Lewis had taken a drawing class and had become interested in clay modeling. When she left Oberlin in early 1863, she did so intending to be a sculptor. She decided to make her career in another antislavery stronghold—Boston, Massachusetts.

Lewis's friends in Oberlin provided her with introductions into Boston's abolitionist and art worlds. She quickly made the acquaintance of several of the city's abolitionists and women's rights activists. A letter from William Lloyd Garrison introduced her to the white sculptor Edward A. Brackett, and she studied with him for a time. She had seen Brackett's stunning bust of John Brown and had concluded that "the man who made a bust of John Brown must be a friend to my people." In Boston, Lewis also received some instruction from the white sculptor Anne Whitney and came to know Harriet Hosmer, one of the first American women to gain fame as a sculptor.

With financial assistance from her brother, Lewis maintained a small workshop in the Studio Building on Tremont Street. She specialized in clay medallions of John Brown and other abolitionists—items she knew would sell at antislavery fairs, one of the few venues that allowed black artists a chance to sell their work. (None of the medallions are known to have survived.)

Lewis also sculpted a likeness of Colonel Robert Gould Shaw. Shaw was the white commander of the Union Army's first black regiment raised in the north, the Massachusetts Fifty-fourth, which had two of Frederick Douglass's sons, Lewis and Charles, in its ranks. Abolitionists heaped praise upon Colonel Shaw: when white officers who commanded black troops were captured, they could be treated as brutally as black prisoners of war.

In late May 1863, Edmonia Lewis was among the cheering crowd of antislavery Bostonians who turned out for the Fifty-fourth's farewell parade. A few months later, she mourned when news spread of the Fifty-fourth's valiant but doomed charge on South Carolina's Battery Wagner. Of the regiment's six hundred soldiers, nearly half were captured, wounded, or killed. Douglass's sons were among the survivors; Colonel Shaw was among the dead.

Working from memory and a few photographs, Lewis made a plaster bust of Shaw. It was highly praised, and she decided to make many more for the Soldier's Relief Fund Fair in the fall of 1864. This event was held to raise money for black soldiers who, though promised, were not receiving the same pay as white soldiers. Edmonia enjoyed the praise and success she achieved during this time; she also made friends and found colleagues.

Lewis sold about one hundred busts of Shaw at the Soldier's Relief Fund Fair. Her success spurred her to heed advice she had received from several people: Go to Florence, Italy—the city that fostered the sixteenth-century master Michelangelo, whose masterpieces include the statue *David* and the frescoed ceiling of the Sistine Chapel in Rome. Edmonia learned a great deal of her craft by copying masterworks by others, including Michelangelo's *Moses*.

Edmonia Lewis arrived in Florence in late 1865, but her work did not sell well there. After a few months she decided to try her luck in Rome, where she had ever increasing success selling her work, and enjoyed some positive critiques in newspapers. She also received moral support from fellow artists Anne Whitney and Harriet Hosmer, who had also relocated to Rome.

Whereas Lewis was initially limited to working with inexpensive materials (clay and plaster), in time she had the funds and the skills to work in marble, the traditional medium of choice for sculptors. One of Lewis's first marble works was *Forever Free*, celebrating the early days of black freedom from bondage. The sculpture features a woman on bended knee, hands clasped and close to her heart, eyes looking skyward, presumably in gratitude. By the woman's side stands a man, eyes also uplifted, broken shackles dangling from one wrist. Lewis also paid tribute to her Native American heritage in several sculptures. One of them is *Old Arrow Maker*.

The Death of Cleopatra is one of Lewis's monumental works. While she was still in Boston, Lewis followed the norms of neoclassicism. Her portrait bust of Robert Gould Shaw portrays him as clear-eyed, intelligent, and serenely

OLD ARROW MAKER
MODELED 1866, CARVED 1872
BY EDMONIA LEWIS
MARBLE
21 1/2 X 13 5/8 X 13 3/8 IN.

A man and a young woman, both dressed in skins, pause for a moment from their work. These are characters from Henry Wadsworth Longfellow's popular epic poem, "The Song of Hiawatha," published in 1855. In the story, the warrior Hiawatha appears at the wigwam of Minnehaha and offers a deer as a token in marriage. Lewis has followed the poet's description and shows Minnehaha "plaiting mats of flags and rushes" and her father "making arrowheads of jasper." They both look toward Hiawatha, whose presence is implied by the deer lying at Minnehaha's feet. Edmonia Lewis executed several copies of the work, which is also known by the title *Hiawatha's Wooing.*

heroic. While in Florence, she met Hiram Powers and Thomas Ball, both important American neoclassical sculptors. Her work developed in response to their influences and the evolving neoclassical style. Her *Cleopatra* is radically different from the Shaw portrait. Lewis presents the betrayed Egyptian queen after she has committed suicide—with all the evidence of love, anger, and

THE DEATH OF CLEOPATRA
CARVED 1876
BY EDMONIA LEWIS
MARBLE
63 X 31 1/4 X 46 IN.

Edmonia Lewis probably began working on the clay model for *The Death of Cleopatra* in 1874 and finished it in 1875. For this large work, she employed Italian craftsmen to translate her model into marble; they completed it in early 1876. Numerous European sculptors had already portrayed the illustrious Cleopatra, though many of those depictions idealized the queen's beauty and her grave calm as she contemplated suicide. Lewis's more realistic and emotionally charged version shows Cleopatra's body racked by death. She rests on her stately throne, dressed in her royal attire and wearing the crown of Egypt. As with images by other artists of the day, the sculpture is a mixture of Greek, Roman, Egyptian, and pseudo-Egyptian details; the hieroglyphics are in fact undecipherable.

despair in full view—slumped on her throne, her head thrown back, the deadly asp still in her hand.

This dramatic *Cleopatra* was one of several sculptures Lewis brought to America for exhibition at the Centennial Exposition, held in celebration of the one-hundredth anniversary of the Declaration of Independence. The Exposition opened in mid-May 1876 in Philadelphia, America's first capital. It covered two hundred acres of Fairmount Park. Nearly two hundred buildings were constructed for the grandest world's fair ever seen.

Some people were appalled by Lewis's *Cleopatra*. One white American artist, William J. Clark, called the sculpture "absolutely repellant." Others applauded it. Writer J. S. Ingram called it "the most remarkable piece of sculpture in the American section." When the Exposition was over, *Cleopatra* remained in America, while Edmonia Lewis returned to Rome. Though she chose Rome, the Canadian artist Edward Mitchell Bannister, another prizewinner at the Exposition, remained in America despite the discrimination he endured.

Like Edmonia Lewis, Edward Bannister was an orphan. During his childhood in St. Andrews, New Brunswick, Bannister supported himself by doing farm chores for a local lawyer. He loved to draw, and his sketches were found on fences, barn doors, and elsewhere around the farm. When Bannister grew up, he worked as a sailor before settling in Boston in the late 1840s, where he supported himself as a barber. By then, art was more than a pastime. He took drawing classes at Lowell Institute in the evenings. During this period he met and married the part-black, part-Narragansett Christiana Carteaux. She was a successful businesswoman, owning several hair salons. She was also a prominent social figure who organized the Soldier's Relief Fund Fair.

Thanks to Christiana's connections within the black middle class, Bannister's paintings were seen and began to sell. The physician John V. De Grasse commissioned a portrait of himself, and that com-

EDWARD MITCHELL BANNISTER
(1828–1901)

OAK TREES
1876
BY EDWARD MITCHELL BANNISTER
OIL ON CANVAS
33 7/8 X 60 1/4 IN.

Edward Mitchell Bannister was unusual among black nineteenth-century American painters in that he achieved recognition and respect without traveling to Europe. The irony in this is that though he remained in New England, his work shows such powerful influence from a group of French painters including Jean-Baptiste-Camille Corot, Jean-François Millet, and Charles-François Daubigny. These painters left Paris to paint outdoors in the village of Barbizon. Bannister's American landscapes similarly show his close observation of and reverence for nature.

In this scene, anchored by two massive oaks, a boatman with his oars over his shoulder strides down the path toward the water. Cattle graze beneath a cloudy sky tinged with blue, a color which is reflected in the blue coat tossed over the boat's gunwale.

commission led to others.

In the late 1860s, the Bannisters decided to move to Providence, Rhode Island, not far from North Kingston, where Christiana had been born. In Providence, Christiana continued to operate her hair salons and Edward continued to paint what was by then his passion: not people, but nature. He painted mesmerizing sunsets and sunrises, pastures, expansive oak trees, placid seaside scenes, and cloud-filled skies.

Bannister's friend George Whitaker described Bannister's paintings as "poems of peace." Whitaker, a white artist and art collector, worked with Bannister to found the Providence Art Club in 1880 to heighten art appreciation.

By the 1880s, Bannister's talent would be recognized beyond New England. Like Edmonia Lewis, his artwork was displayed at the Centennial Exposition of 1876: a landscape listed in the catalog as "No. 54." This painting, *Under the Oaks,* won a certificate of award and first-place medal for oil paintings, making Bannister the first black artist in America to receive an important award at a major art exhibition. Not long after the Centennial, *Under the Oaks* sold for fifteen hundred dollars, which could buy then what about twenty-five thousand dollars can buy today. Its whereabouts are now unknown.

Bannister's thrill at winning such an important prize must have been soured by the way he was treated when he tried to confirm his win.

"I hurried to the committee room to make sure the report was true. A great crowd was there ahead of me, and as I jostled through this many resented my presence, some actually commenting within my hearing, in a most petulant manner asking, 'Why is this colored person here?'"

When Bannister finally reached the inquiry desk, the man behind it ignored him. Then, "without more than raising his eyes he demanded in a most exasperating tone of voice, 'Well, what do you want here anyway? Speak lively.'"

"I want to inquire concerning fifty-four." Bannister replied. "Is it a prize winner?"

what's that to you?" the man snapped.

Bannister was livid, but he did not explode. As he told Whitaker, "Controlling myself, I said with deliberation, 'I am interested in the report that *Under the Oaks* has received a prize. I painted that picture.'"

The disrespect Bannister experienced was typical. Even though by the time of the Centennial slavery had been abolished, blacks had been granted citizenship, and black men had gained the right to the national vote, antiblack sentiment still reigned. Furthermore, the vast majority of blacks had to contend with segregation—limiting where they could live, work, have a meal, and go to school. Bannister chose to remain in America despite these facts, but such persistent prejudice certainly drove scores of talented artists to Europe. Painter Henry Ossawa Tanner was one of many who spent most of his life away from America.

Henry Tanner was born in Pennsylvania's Allegheny City (long since a part of Pittsburgh) and spent most of his youth in Philadelphia. Henry's father, Reverend Benjamin Tucker Tanner, hoped his first-born would become a minister. When Henry was thirteen, however, he spotted an artist at work on a landscape during a walk with his father in the hills of Fairmount Park. Young Henry watched the artist capture life on canvas for about an hour. He was utterly fascinated, and began to envision himself as an artist. The next day, with fifteen cents he had wheedled from his parents, Henry purchased some cheap paint and, as he later put it, "a couple of scraggy brushes." Improvising on the rest of a painter's gear—a piece of awning for a canvas, the cover of an

HENRY OSSAWA TANNER
(1859–1937)

ABRAHAM'S OAK
1905
BY HENRY OSSAWA
TANNER
OIL ON CANVAS
21 3/8 X 28 5/8 IN.

Henry Ossawa Tanner, with his close knowledge of the Bible, did not paint illustrations of its stories, but used the text as a point of departure. In this work, a sturdy oak on a grassy plain dwarfs a handful of trees and shrubs and two mysterious human figures who stand in close conversation. The entire scene is bathed in brilliant moonlight. The biblical patriarch Abraham was the father of the twelve tribes of Israel through his son Isaac, and the father of Islam through his son Ishmael. When he was seventy-five years old, Abraham set out from Haran and traveled to Canaan (the lowlands of Palestine) at the Lord's command. This painting represents the grove of trees Abraham was said to have planted at Beersheba, Palestine's first permanent place of worship (Genesis 21:33).

old textbook for a palette—Henry returned to Fairmount Park and went to work on his first landscape.

"Coming home that night," he later recounted, "I examined the sketch from all points of view, upside down and downside up, decidedly admiring and well content with my first effort." This first painting was followed by a second, a third, and a fourth—young Tanner made "effort" after "effort," year after year. How wonderful for him that in 1876 the Centennial Exposition came to his hometown! Tanner had six whole months to take in thousands of works of art. There was art from England, France, Italy, and other nations. There was art by hundreds of white Americans, including paintings by the celebrated Gilbert Stuart, Winslow Homer, and Thomas Eakins. And there were the two works by black artists: Edmonia Lewis's *The Death of Cleopatra* and Edward Bannister's *Under the Oaks*.

By the time of the exhibition, Tanner was fixed on being a professional artist. He had trouble finding someone to teach him, so he taught himself by studying paintings in books and by looking at art in shops and galleries—and by painting constantly.

In 1880, twenty-year-old Tanner's discipline and determination paid off: He enrolled in Philadelphia's Pennsylvania Academy of the Fine Arts, America's premier art school at the time. Only one other black person—Robert Douglass Jr. of Philadelphia—had attended the academy since its founding in 1805.

At the academy, Tanner studied photography and painting with Thomas Eakins, who had been enrolled at the École des Beaux Arts (School of Fine Arts) in Paris, regarded as the finest art school in the world. Eakins, who later became director of the academy, was a strong advocate of realism, wherein an artist presents a field, bowl of apples, or a face as it is—not as he or she remembers it, imagines it, or fantasizes it to be. Tanner, who idolized Eakins, diligently practiced what his teacher preached.

THE BANJO LESSON
1893
BY HENRY OSSAWA TANNER
OIL ON CANVAS
49 X 35 1/2 IN.

The scene is set in a room where the heat of a cooking fire from a stone hearth and a soft glowing light warm the figures. A barefoot boy stands on a plank floor between the knees of a gray-haired man. The boy's arms are wrapped around a banjo that is too big for him to hold himself; the man's hand helps to support the instrument's neck. They may have paused in the midst of other tasks for an impromptu music lesson; a coffee pot and skillet rest near the fire and a hat and pipe have been dropped on the floor. This is a purely secular genre scene, but the shimmering light that rakes across the wall, the tablecloth, and the dishes will reappear when Henry Ossawa Tanner turns to religious subjects.

For Tanner, studying with Eakins was a terrific experience, but his relations with some fellow students were terrible. He had to contend with the silent treatment, racial slurs, and worse. One evening, a group of students dragged him, along with his easel, out into the street and staged a "crucifix-ion," tying Tanner to his easel and leaving him there alone to struggle free.

Tanner eventually gave up on further studies at the academy, but not on being an artist. He continued to paint, primarily landscapes and seascapes. In time, he found patrons who purchased his paintings so that he could afford to keep working. His parents continued to support him and eventually Tanner had enough money to study in Europe. In early January 1891, Tanner was on his way to Rome. But during a stopover in Paris, he decided to stay there and enroll in one of that city's many arts schools, the Académie Julian.

In France, Tanner did not experience the silent treatment or torment. Instead, he enjoyed vibrant conversations with artists of many nationalities. He also received tremendous encouragement from the award-winning painter Jean Joseph Benjamin-Constant, one of the school's most respected instructors.

In the spring of 1892, Tanner discovered something new to strive for when he happened upon a prestigious annual art show: Le Salon de la Société des Artistes Français—Le Salon (the Salon) for short. Tanner set his sights on having a painting accepted in the Salon. Such a stamp of approval would greatly increase his standing as an artist.

The Salon rejected the first painting Tanner submitted, but he was determined to submit again. But before he could do so, he was stricken with typhoid fever and was hospitalized. Since his youth, Tanner had always been physically frail. It did not help that while in Paris he spent hours at the easel, often skimping on food and sleep.

After his release from the hospital, Tanner returned to Philadelphia to recuperate in his parents' home. As soon as he recovered, he was back at his easel. It was during these days that Tanner created two of his best-known paintings: *The Banjo Lesson* and *The Thankful Poor*. Both depict an older black man and a young boy, in one case making music, and in the other saying grace

STUDY FOR THE
RAISING OF LAZARUS
ABOUT 1895–1897
BY HENRY OSSAWA
TANNER
OIL ON PLYWOOD
6 X 7 7/8 IN.

Henry Ossawa Tanner was less interested in portraying realistic scenes of the Holy Land than in capturing the spirituality that infused his own life. Not for him the triumphant saints and angels or the beautiful Madonnas with chubby infants, but rather translucent figures illuminated from within by faith and hope. He worked for months on *The Raising of Lazarus,* completing study after study before he found just the right composition and lighting.

over a meal. Perhaps Tanner's return to the city of his youth prompted him to try his hand at "genre painting," as such scenes of everyday life are known.

Discrimination against blacks was still intense in the 1890s, and Tanner was desperate to return to France where he felt so free. He sold as many paintings as he could to finance his trip, and in Paris he had much more than a sense of freedom to celebrate.

The Salon of 1894 accepted Tanner's *The Banjo Lesson*. The following year, the Salon accepted not one, but two of his paintings, and one pastel. It was around this time that Tanner began painting more and more biblical scenes.

Daniel in the Lion's Den, Tanner's first biblical painting, was not only accepted but also received an honorable mention at the Salon of 1896. The next year, Tanner's *The Raising of Lazarus* received a third-place medal. The French government purchased *Lazarus* for its esteemed Musée de Luxembourg (Museum of Luxembourg). Only a few American artists had ever received that honor.

Tanner's triumphs in France sparked increased interest in his work— among art critics, gallery owners, museum curators, and art collectors in both Europe and America. At the end of the nineteenth century, Tanner was the most celebrated black American artist. The story of his talent and tenacity became a beacon for scores of black artists who would strive to make their mark in the twentieth century.

Robert Scott Duncanson

(1821/1822–1872)

The body of the raptor, perched on the summit of a crag, is bowed in a tense arc as it plucks brilliant feathers from the silenced songbird. Buildings top the distant cliffs and the scene is surmounted by a storm-darkened sky. The birds embody the power of life and the poignancy of death and are captured by the artist's brush just as the struggle has ceased. This scene of simultaneous victory and defeat conveys the power and majesty of nature as surely as Robert Scott Duncanson's more widely known sun-drenched landscapes and rainbows.

By the time he painted this picture, Duncanson would certainly have been aware of the work of the famous naturalist painter John James Audubon and his famous book, *Birds of America.* The two artists had a great deal in common. Audubon was of mixed race—he was born in Haiti to a French naval officer and a Creole mother, and his work as a naturalist had brought him to Ohio and Kentucky over the course of many years. Duncanson, who was born in Fayette, New York, was the son of a black woman and a Scottish man. In the early 1840s he moved to Mount Healthy, not far from Cincinnati, Ohio. Although the city was on the frontier in the mid-nineteenth century, it was no cultural desert. Duncanson would have seen works by Thomas Cole, Asher Durand, and other American artists exhibited there.

Vulture and Its Prey
1844
BY ROBERT SCOTT DUNCANSON
OIL ON CANVAS
27 1/8 X 22 1/4 IN.

I Baptize Thee (detail)
ABOUT 1940
BY WILLIAM H. JOHNSON
OIL ON BURLAP
38 1/8 X 45 1/2 IN.

GREAT AWAKENINGS

P rogress! As Americans strode into a new century, legions of workers pressed corporate bosses for better wages and treatment. Troops of women lobbied the government for the right to the national vote, which was finally secured in 1920.

It was a time of innovation, as inventions, such as the vacuum cleaner, the radio, Will Keith Kellogg's Corn Flakes, Crayola crayons, and movies, first silent then with sound, changed the way people lived. Fascination with air travel flared following Wilbur and Orville Wright's 1903 breakthrough with their "aeroplane" at Kitty Hawk, North Carolina. And Henry Ford's relatively afford-able Model T would soon have an ever-growing number of Americans on the road. Black Americans were on the move, too.

MALVIN GRAY JOHNSON
(1896–1934)

Malvin Gray Johnson, who was born in Greensboro, North Carolina, but spent most of his life in New York City, painted this self-portrait in 1934, the year of his death. Johnson was not merely portraying himself as a stereotypical brooding artist. Behind his likeness, there is a painting of two African masks—similar to a still life he created in 1932. Portraits usually show their subjects with props or backgrounds that detail the sitter's profession, personality, or values.

SELF-PORTRAIT
1934
BY MALVIN GRAY JOHNSON
OIL ON CANVAS MOUNTED ON CANVAS
38 1/4 X 30 IN.

The majority of black Americans had always lived in the South. In the early twentieth century, however, many of them migrated to midwestern and northern cities in search of better-paying jobs in factories, hotels, and on the railroad. While it is true that they were migrating toward better economic opportunity, they were also fleeing the social conditions of the South, where lynchings and other acts of violence by white supremacist groups such as the Ku Klux Klan continued. These were some of the motivating factors in what became known as the Great Migration.

A number of civil rights organizations gathered momentum, waging campaigns against segregation and other forms of discrimination. The interracial National Association for the Advancement of Colored People (NAACP) was one such group. One of its cofounders, the Harvard-educated historian and sociologist William Edward Burghardt (W. E. B.) Du Bois, launched the NAACP's dynamic magazine, *The Crisis*. While exposing injustices and rallying people against discrimination, *The Crisis* cheered black achievement in everything from the sciences to the arts through articles, competitions, and awards. Doing so, W. E. B. Du Bois and others reasoned, would inspire more blacks to positive ambitions and more whites to stop thinking of blacks as mentally inferior. It was time to stamp out old notions of black people as good for nothing but servanthood. That was the message delivered by this upsurge of black pride and activism, dubbed the New Negro Movement. (At the time "Negro" was considered more dignified than "colored" and other terms often used to refer to black people.)

Alain Locke, America's first black Rhodes Scholar and a professor of philosophy at Washington, D.C.'s Howard University compiled the movement's manifesto: *The New Negro* (1925). This anthology of fiction, poetry, drama, and song offered groundbreaking essays, such as "The Negro Digs Up His Past," a call for deeper research into and wider teaching of black history. The essay's author was the Afro–Puerto Rican bibliophile Arturo Alfonso Schomburg, whose collection of art, books, and memorabilia became the core of the New York Public Library's Negro division in Harlem, on 135th Street (genesis of the Schomburg Center for Research in Black Culture).

In his essay "The Legacy of the Ancestral Arts," Locke exhorted black visual artists to look to black African art for inspiration. "African sculpture has been for contemporary European painting and sculpture just such a mine of fresh motifs," Locke pointed out. The Spanish painter Pablo Picasso was among the dozens of artists Locke included in his list of examples. Picasso had found in masks of the Dogon people of Mali partial inspiration for his abstract style of painting called "cubism" (named for its heavy reliance on geometric shapes). While Locke respected Henry Tanner, he challenged young artists to do what Tanner and others had done only occasionally: namely, feature black life and culture in their work.

Like Locke, many of the "new negroes" did not live in Harlem. But because Du Bois, Schomburg, and other notables did, and because Harlem was regarded as the "capital" of black America, the New Negro movement's artistic wing (from literature to the performing and visual arts) became commonly called the "Harlem Renaissance."

What matters is not the name, but the fact that in the first few decades of the twentieth century black artists made progress. Discrimination persisted, but so did they. More visual artists than before reached for opportunities to study art in America and abroad. More awakened to their history and reached into their own lives and heritage for subjects to portray. More explored an array of styles and moved beyond the concept of art as an imitation (or copy) of life, and into the modern view of art as an expression of an artist's perspective and feelings about life. Black artists and intellectuals came to feel that they were participating in a momentous change. Augusta Savage, one of

James VanDerZee

(1886–1983)

This studio portrait shows a young woman in a fine beaded dress, her graceful arms loosely cradling the flowers. Her eyes fall away and to our left, as though her thoughts have strayed from the present.

If there was an "official photographer" for the New Negro movement, it was James VanDerZee. After a happy New England childhood, he moved to New York in 1905 and gravitated to Harlem in 1908. By 1916 he had met the woman who would be his second wife, and together they opened the Guarantee Photo Studio on West 135th Street.

When he was not making portraits, VanDerZee ventured out into the community, photographing shops, parades, weddings, church groups, and sports teams.

He was swept into the politics of the New Negro movement, and during the 1920s he was commissioned by Marcus Garvey to document the activities of the Universal Negro Improvement Association. Hundreds of images show rallies, parades, and dignitaries on reviewing stands draped with bunting.

Evening Attire
1922
by James VanDerZee
gelatin silver print
on paper mounted
on paperboard
10 x 8 in.

Augusta Savage (1900–1962) in her studio with her sculpture *Realization*, about 1938.

the leading artists of the New Negro movement, sculpted a statue that, though now lost, probably embodied that idea. It was called *The New Negro,* and was described as a black man "kneeling in a fetal position."

Augusta Savage made a long journey from her childhood to her central place in the Harlem Renaissance. She was only about six years old when she started playing with some of the rich, red clay so abundant in her northern Florida hometown of Green Cove Springs. First, little Augusta fashioned a duck, then a family of ducks, then other animals. She was one of the fourteen children born to her parents, who had a hard time making ends meet; her creations were her toys.

Savage's childhood play developed into a serious career after 1921. She was in her late twenties and had less than five dollars to her name when she moved to New York City. She settled in Harlem and enrolled in a school in downtown Manhattan.

That school was the Cooper Union, established in the late 1850s by Peter Cooper, a wealthy, white real estate developer and philanthropist. Cooper was a self-taught chemist and engineer, inventor, and abolitionist. Cooper, born poor, had little formal education in his youth. To help those who would follow him, he founded the Cooper Union, which was the nation's first free institution of higher learning.

Savage advanced through the Cooper Union's four-year sculpture course in three years (supporting herself largely through domestic work). While she studied, she met a variety of people in Harlem who consequently discovered her talent. Her reputation spread beyond Harlem after she ended up in the news.

"Negress Denied Entry to French Art School," read a headline in the *New York Times* in April 1923. The French government was offering scholarships to one hundred American women for a summer of study at a school in Fontainebleau, near Paris. The committee of white American men in charge of the applications rejected Savage because she was black. For the committee,

GAMIN
ABOUT 1929
BY AUGUSTA SAVAGE
PAINTED PLASTER
9 X 5 3/4 X 4 3/8 IN.

Traditionally, sculptors made portraits of famous people or wealthy patrons. Augusta Savage turned this tradition upside down with her bust of an ordinary boy. In doing so, Savage affirmed the dignity of the everyday black American. The perceptive sculptor created tensions of class as well as race. This work was cast in bronze, an expensive, exclusive medium that contrasts with the informally dressed sitter. Savage modeled clay expertly in the wrinkles of *Gamin*'s cap and shirt and in his realistic facial features. The sitter's unapologetic gaze, cast past the viewer, conveys his tough yet vulnerable assurance. In this powerful work, Savage's passion for racial equality manifests in a natural, subtle, and appealing way.

"American women" meant "white American women." The committee feared the presence of a black woman might offend other applicants.

The publicity Savage received around this rejection won her many supporters. Several people commissioned sculptures of black heroes. One of Savage's first commissions was for a bust of W. E. B. Du Bois, which would be installed in the 135th Street library. Savage also sculpted a portrait of Marcus Garvey; her husband, Robert Poston, was one of Garvey's aides. Garvey, the Jamaican-born, Harlem-based founder of the Universal Negro Improvement Association, was a powerful voice calling for blacks to embrace their African heritage; he even advocated that they move to Africa. Garvey also urged blacks to have as little to do with white people as possible. Savage did not agree with the whole of Garvey's philosophy, but she did admire him to a certain extent (and also contributed poetry to his newspaper, *The Negro World*).

Ironically, Savage won the highest praise for a sculpture not of a hero, but of an everyday boy. *Gamin,* which may have been modeled on Savage's nephew, appeared on the cover of *Opportunity,* the magazine of the National Urban League, another interracial civil rights organization. The Urban League's chief, Eugene Kinckle Jones, and a Harlem real-estate broker, John Nail, who had purchased one of Savage's sculptures, became her loyal supporters. The two men lobbied for Savage to receive a fellowship from the Rosenwald Foundation, established by Julius Rosenwald, head of the mail-order house, Sears, Roebuck and Company. The grant allowed Savage to study art for a year in Paris, at that time the art capital of the world.

In September 1929—a month before the stock market crash that triggered the Great Depression—Augusta Savage sailed to France. There, she studied for a time with master sculptor Benneteau-Degrois (learning French along the way) and produced many sculptures, mostly statues of women evincing strength. Thanks to a second Rosenwald fellowship and a grant from the Carnegie Foundation (established by the steel magnate Andrew Carnegie), Savage extended her stay in Europe, expanding her knowledge by studying sculpture in museums and cathedrals in Belgium and Germany.

When Augusta Savage returned to America in 1932, the country was still in the grip of the Great Depression. Savage persevered with her art. Much of it would consist of busts of prominent people, among them writer, diplomat, and activist James Weldon Johnson, who wrote the lyrics to "Lift Every Voice and Sing," which became the Negro national anthem.

After her return to America, Savage channeled her energies into helping other blacks develop their artistic talent. She continued to receive grants, including another from the Carnegie Foundation. She used the money to open the Savage Studio of Arts and Crafts in Harlem, a place where local children could study art and learn more about black culture at no cost.

Savage sought funding from many sources to expand the studio; she won grants from several Harlem-based organizations as well as funding from the Works Projects Administration (WPA), a government agency that created jobs for a multitude of men and women during the Depression. The WPA employed millions in major construction projects (buildings, bridges, roads) around the nation. The government also created an entirely new environment for the arts in America when it hired legions of literary, performing, and visual artists to create public works of art through the WPA's Federal Writers' Project, Federal Theatre Project, and Federal Arts Project.

Augusta Savage's Studio morphed into the Uptown Art Laboratory, and finally, in 1937, into the Harlem Community Art Center. There, people of all ages studied pottery, weaving, photography, printmaking, painting, sculpting, and other arts. Along with the 135th Street library, the Harlem Community Art Center was one of the few places in New York City where black artists could exhibit their work and thereby increase their chances of receiving sales and commissions.

Augusta Savage was also a key figure in the Harlem Artists Guild. Through the Guild, artists aided one another with everything from finding a place to live to loans. The Guild mounted exhibits in churches and other spaces in Harlem, organized lectures, and lobbied for equality in the way government

*LIFT EVERY VOICE
AND SING*
1939
BY AUGUSTA
SAVAGE
PAINTED PLASTER
16 FT. HIGH

*Lift Every Voice
and Sing* was
extremely popular
at the 1939
World's Fair, and
was reproduced
on postcards and
in a variety of
smaller plaster
versions to be sold
as souvenirs.

projects were funded. The Guild had played a pivotal role in the creation of the Harlem Community Art Center.

Many people who passed through Savage's art school became accomplished artists. They include painter Norman Lewis, sculptor and painter Gwendolyn Knight, and the painter she married, Jacob Lawrence. "If I can inspire one of these youngsters to develop the talent I know they possess," Savage once said of her students, "then my monument will be their work. No one could ask more than that."

Augusta Savage created about seventy-five sculptures. *The New Negro* is only one of many that did not survive. Another terrible loss, *Lift Every Voice and Sing*, featured a line of black children with their mouths open in song. Their bodies are the strings of a harp, and a mighty forearm is the harp's base. A boy holding a plaque with musical notes kneels in front of the singing children. Savage was commissioned to create the work, a tribute to African American contributions to music, for the 1939–40 World's Fair (held in Flushing Meadows, New York). The massive, black-lacquered plaster statue was known as *Lift Every Voice and Sing* because Savage took that song as her inspiration. After the fair, a wrecking crew bulldozed the sculpture along with everything else in the temporary building where it had been displayed. It would have been expensive to move and store such a large piece, and Savage did not have the money.

The Rosenwald and the Carnegie foundations, so helpful to Savage, were not the only white philanthropic organizations to encourage and celebrate black achievement. The Harmon Foundation, established by the real-estate developer William Elmer Harmon, had an annual competition resulting in "Awards for Distinguished Achievement Among Negroes." As important as it was for children to be able to study art, if they were to continue to be artists as adults, it was also important that their achievements be publicly recognized. Initially, the Harmon Foundation offered awards in several fields, but beginning in 1930, they were limited to the visual arts.

The first competition took place in 1926, and Palmer Hayden and Hale Woodruff received the first visual arts awards. Hayden's watercolor of a Maine seascape won the gold medal; Woodruff's oil painting of two elderly black women radiating wisdom and dignity won the bronze. On the heels of their Harmon wins, both painters journeyed to France where, despite their radically different tastes, temperaments, and interests, they became friends.

Palmer Hayden, born in the tiny town of Widewater, Virginia, was the fifth of ten children. Like many other artists, Hayden showed an interest in art at a young age. Early encouragement came from a teacher. "Keep at it," the woman said, "and you'll be a famous artist."

Young Palmer's first fascination had not been painting, but the violin. He kept that dream a secret because he was rather shy: He doubted he would ever be able to perform before lots of people. Also, his parents could not afford to buy him a violin. As his dream of being a musician faded, his love for art intensified.

Palmer was nearly eighteen when he left home in search of work. He ended up in Washington, D.C., where he found a job in a drugstore cleaning up and running errands. In his spare time he drew, mostly scenes of life on the Potomac River. The more he drew, the more he longed to make a living as an artist. He did not see how he could afford to go to art school, so Hayden placed an ad in a local paper: "Young artist would like a job as an assistant to commercial artist." Naturally, Hayden was thrilled

PALMER HAYDEN
(1890–1973)

THE JANITOR WHO PAINTS
ABOUT 1937
BY PALMER HAYDEN
OIL ON CANVAS
39 1/8 X 32 7/8 IN.

This painting may be a tribute to Palmer Hayden's friend, Cloyde Boykin, who was both a janitor and a painter. But Hayden the artist, who also worked as a janitor, is telling us about himself as well. The artist in this picture is probably painting his portrait of a woman and her baby in the "super's apartment" that comes with his day job. It is not a luxurious home—hot water pipes hang from the ceiling and a bare lightbulb offers the only light, but a red cloth on the bedside table brightens the corner, and a portrait of the cat hangs on the wall. The artist is surrounded by the tools of both his trades—painter and janitor. The prominent clock shows the time as ten past five. Having hung up his broom and feather duster for the day, he has not allowed a moment to pass before he is fully absorbed by the painting in front of him. The janitor is just beginning his second shift.

when an artist responded to his ad, requesting an interview. Hayden's hope was short-lived, however: "When he saw me, he said, 'Oh, I didn't know you were colored,' and closed the door and that ended the interview."

Hayden did not allow that incident to crush his hope of being an artist. Neither did he stay in Washington. Hayden did not stay anywhere for very long:

He moved from city to city, from job to job. He was a roustabout with the Ringling Brothers Circus, a carter at a brickyard in upstate New York, a sandhog in Boston, a mate on an oyster boat on the Chesapeake Bay, and a construction worker in New York City. Hayden also served two tours of duty in the then segregated U.S. Army: first with the Twenty-fourth Infantry in the Philippines (an American territory at the time) and then, during World War I, with the Tenth Cavalry at West Point. Wherever he was, Hayden painted the people and events around him—from circus acts like the Frog Man (a contortionist), to his fellow soldiers, to scenes of Filipino life.

When Hayden mustered out of the army in 1920, he settled in New York City's Greenwich Village, where many artists lived and worked. He enrolled in a summer course at Columbia University, which was the first formal training he had ever had. He built on what he learned there through brief study at the Cooper Union and, in the summer of 1925, he worked at an art colony in Boothbay Harbor, Maine, exchanging his labor for lessons.

During much of this time, Hayden eked out a living cleaning people's apartments. One of his clients, a wealthy white woman named Alice Dike, discovered Hayden was an artist and gave him a brochure she had picked up at her church. This brochure announced the 1926 Harmon Foundation art competition. At the woman's urging, Hayden entered three paintings.

With the four-hundred-dollar cash award that came with the gold medal and a hefty gift of three thousand dollars from Alice Dike, in March 1927 Hayden set sail for France, where he lived for six years.

After so many years of living on so little, Hayden could not resist the temptation to splurge. He bought expensive clothes and went to nightclubs. Despite his extravagances and late nights, he produced sketches, watercolors, and oils, primarily of Paris delights.

Through discussions with other artists about cubism and other modern art styles, Hayden developed a clearer vision of himself as an artist. "Cubism and that sort of painting,"

JOHN HENRY ON THE RIGHT,
STEAM DRILL ON THE LEFT
1944–1947
BY PALMER HAYDEN
OIL ON CANVAS
30 X 40 IN.

As a child, Palmer Hayden knew that John Henry was a legendary figure of song and story. During his adulthood, he discovered that John Henry was a real person who had worked on the Chesapeake and Ohio Railroad and had helped carve out the mile-long tunnel at Big Bend on the Greenbriar River. In the ballad about John Henry, the folk hero agrees to pit his strength with a hammer against a man with a steam drill. He wins the competition, but the effort is too much, and "he dies with his hammer in his hand."

Hayden made many artworks in which he portrayed black people with exaggerated features. Many of his peers resented such work because they felt Hayden was promoting stereotypes.

MIDNIGHT AT THE
CROSSROADS
ABOUT 1940
BY PALMER HAYDEN
OIL ON CANVAS
28 X 34 IN.

Palmer Hayden often painted dreams and made a special effort to render them faithfully. Here, a young boy stands at a fork in the road, holding a violin and a bow that are too big for his slight body. To the right, the road stretches back to a local church and perhaps other familiar things. The road on the left, though brightly lit by the moonlight, curves around and into the trees, putting any destination beyond our sight. Hayden had longed to play the violin as a child, but an instrument was beyond his parents' means. Years later he dreamed of this boy at the crossroads. It seemed to represent his choice to find his artistic life even though he had been unable to pursue his dreams of music.

Hayden once remarked, "I never was interested in because I couldn't tell a story."

After he returned to America in the early 1930s, Hayden remained true to his passion for narrative paintings. He continued to paint from his memories, both of his job-jumping days and his childhood. He recalled his father singing "The Ballad of John Henry." The story of this mighty-muscled "steel-drivin' man" inspired Hayden's longest series, the twelve paintings known as "John Henry." One of his most touching paintings, however, is the autobiographical *Midnight at the Crossroads,* in which a young boy with a violin under his arm stands at a fork in a road.

Hayden's fellow Harmon award–winner Hale Woodruff, born in Cairo, Illinois, and raised in Nashville, Tennessee, saw his path at a fairly young age. His mother gave him his first drawing lessons, and he proceeded to tutor himself by copying artwork from newspapers, his mother's illustrated Bible, and his schoolbooks. Young Hale had friends, but as an only child, "there were times when I found myself by myself," he later recalled, "so I'd just sit down and draw." And there were times when he contributed cartoons to his high school newspaper, the *Pearl High Voice,* and times when he feasted his eyes on reproductions of Henry Tanner's paintings in the pages of *The Crisis,* daydreaming of going to France.

After Woodruff graduated from high school, his buddy George Gore proposed a trip. "Come on, let's go up to Indianapolis, I have my family there; we can pass the summer." In Indianapolis, the young men found work as houseboys in a hotel. Seeing an art exhibit at the John Herron Art Institute, Hale decided to stay in Indianapolis and enroll at Herron, which was both an art museum and art school. (It later evolved into two institutions: the Indianapolis Museum of Art and Indiana University's Herron School of Art.)

Woodruff supported himself with a mix of menial jobs. He also earned money drawing political cartoons for the *Indianapolis Ledger,* on lynchings,

GEORGIA LANDSCAPE
ABOUT 1934-1935
BY HALE WOODRUFF
OIL ON CANVAS
21 1/8 X 25 5/8 IN.

In *Georgia Landscape*, the influences of Paul Cézanne and Vincent van Gogh are evident. The bright colors and short brush strokes look like van Gogh's style, while the curving shapes of the trees echo some of Cézanne's famous landscapes. After returning from Paris in 1931, Hale Woodruff settled in Atlanta, a city then teeming with black scholars and artists. In an interview, Woodruff reflected, "These were the Depression days and somehow much of your great talent found itself in Atlanta because there were few other openings for people during the thirties when jobs were scarce and hard to find. But it was fortunate for the beginnings of Atlanta University, and Spelman College, and Morehouse, where this unusual talent and these people congregated." Perhaps this brightly colored undulating landscape refers to Atlanta's climate of bright people and surging ideas as much as it captures the red clay of the outlying countryside.

police brutality, and other social issues of the day.

After a few semesters at Herron, lack of funds forced Woodruff to withdraw. Hoping to find better paying work, he headed for Chicago, where he enrolled in that city's Art Institute. After a short time there, however, he decided to return to Indianapolis. Woodruff painted a large number of landscapes and was able to show them at the annual Indiana Artists Exhibitions at Herron, and at the "colored" YMCA on Senate Avenue, where he lived. He also learned about black history and civil rights work from the YMCA's guest lecturers.

Woodruff became friends with a German man, Hermann Lieber, who ran an art supply store on West Washington Street, and above it, a gallery where he occasionally exhibited Woodruff's paintings. One day Lieber gave Woodruff a present he would cherish forever.

"Woodruff," said Lieber, "I want you to have this book. I want you to take this little book because it records the great work of your great people: African art." The book was *Afrikanische Plastik* (*African Sculpture*) by Carl Einstein, a German art critic (and nephew of physicist Albert Einstein).

"You can't imagine the effect that book had on me," Woodruff told a colleague some fifty years later. "I had never heard of the significance of— the impact of—African art. Yet here it was! All written up in German, a language I didn't understand! Yet published with beautiful photographs and treated with great seriousness and respect! Plainly sculptures of black people, my people, they were considered very beautiful by these German art experts! The whole idea that this could be so was

HALE WOODRUFF
(1900–1980)

like an explosion. It was a real turning point for me."

Woodruff was still enthralled with African art a few years later when he won the Harmon bronze medal. Mary Brady, director of the Harmon Foundation, saw to it that Woodruff received some publicity, both on his win and his desire to go to France. The publicity resulted in small and large donations from individuals and organizations, and in early September 1927, Woodruff was on his way to Paris. Once there, he sought out Palmer Hayden, who helped him get settled.

In Paris, Woodruff allowed himself some fun, spending time with Hayden and other black American artists, writers, and musicians visiting or living in Paris at the time. Unlike Hayden, however, Woodruff did not overdo it. Instead, he engaged in some formal study at two art schools, did a great deal of painting, and soaked up art at museums. "To tell you the truth," he told a writer years later, "I got my art education in the museums. I really credit my influences from seeing all kinds of art and artists in the museums."

That "all kinds of art" included a major exhibition of paintings by the French artist Claude Monet, pioneer of the impressionist movement. Most impressionists tended to use soft colors to create the effect of natural light on a subject. "I had never seen such color before!" Woodruff remarked, recalling that Monet exhibit.

Woodruff repeatedly returned to the Musée de l'Homme (Museum of Mankind) for its exhibit of black African art. "There's always the dignity," he told an interviewer in the late 1960s. "There's always a very great sense of self. And the significance of the self."

Woodruff was thrilled to see Henry Tanner's famous painting *The Raising of Lazarus* in the Musée de Luxembourg. Like almost every other black American who visited France in the 1920s, Woodruff wanted to meet the artist. At the time, Tanner was living in Étaples, a fishing village in northern France.

Afro Emblems
1950
by Hale Woodruff
oil on linen
18 x 22 in.

In 1946, Hale Woodruff left Atlanta for New York City. There, he met artists who explored new styles and ideas. A group called the abstract expressionists tried to convey feelings directly with paint, often using unstructured shapes and colors. In *Afro Emblems*, Woodruff combines abstract art concepts and African symbols.

BACK TO AFRICA
FROM "THE AMISTAD
MURALS"
BY HALE WOODRUFF
1938–1939
OIL ON CANVAS
42 X 78 IN.

Hale Woodruff created several murals. This painting is one of three that make up his "Amistad" series, comissioned for the Savery Library at Talladega College in Alabama. "Amistad" celebrates a group of Africans who mutinied aboard a slave ship in 1839 and several years later were granted the right to return to Africa.

Unlike many murals, the "Amistad" series was not painted on a wall. Woodruff created the works on canvas so that, as a friend put it, "if any had to be taken down, they wouldn't have to be destroyed."

Woodruff spent a memorable day with Tanner, talking about their ideas and about artistic techniques. Woodruff also shared his love for the work of French painter Paul Cézanne, and Tanner applauded. Cézanne, regarded as the father of modern art, had rebelled against the softness and formlessness of impressionist painting. He championed the use of bolder colors. He called for more structure and advanced ideas that gave birth to cubism.

Woodruff was happy in France, but like many artists he was struggling financially. He shipped many paintings to Mary Brady at the Harmon Foundation (as did Palmer Hayden) hoping for sales, but sales were few in both America and France. But Woodruff had no regrets about his time in France.

Shortly after Woodruff returned to America in 1931, he taught at Atlanta University (today Clark Atlanta University). The university's president, John Hope, whose art collection included paintings by Edward Bannister, had purchased a painting from Woodruff years earlier in Indianapolis.

Woodruff was determined to build a strong art department. He also launched an annual exhibition of student work, which blossomed into the Atlanta University Annual Exhibition of Paintings, Sculpture and Prints by Negro Artists, and continued until 1970.

While in Georgia, Woodruff was influenced by regionalism, a style associated with midwestern artists who specialized in rural subjects. Regionalists focused on local scenes and people, imbuing the everyday with a sense of the epic.

Woodruff also fell in love with the work of the Mexican muralists José Clemente Orozco, David Siqueiros, and Diego Rivera—known as *Los Tres Grandes* (The Three Great Ones). These artists brought art to everyday people by creating frescoes on the walls of schools and other public spaces. They understood that ordinary people appreciated and deserved art. They deplored the fact that such people were often intimidated by and made to feel unwelcome in museums and art galleries. Their murals were not only *for* the people, they were also often art *of* the people—portraying the struggles and glories of peasants and low-wage workers, capturing folkways and traditions. The power of their art crossed the border and sparked a vogue for murals in public and private spaces all over America in the 1930s.

Woodruff spent a summer in Mexico, where he apprenticed with Diego Rivera and in time became a master muralist. He painted his best-known series of murals for the library at Alabama's Talladega College. The detailed, dense, and boldly colored "Amistad" murals recount the courage of the kidnapped Mende prince Sengbe (also known as Cinque) and other Africans aboard the Spanish slave ship *La Amistad* (*Friendship*). After the Africans took over the ship, they were tried in America for piracy. Defended by former president John Quincy Adams and eventually set free, they returned to their homeland in present-day Sierra Leone. Woodruff completed these murals in 1939, the one-hundredth anniversary of the uprising aboard *La Amistad*.

Shortly before Woodruff finished the "Amistad" murals, *Life* magazine got wind of the project and sent the acclaimed Latvian-American photographer Eliot Elisofon to do a photodocumentary on Woodruff and his work. A feature story in *Life,* the world's leading picture magazine, would definitely have boosted his career.

Elisofon spent several days with Woodruff, but the story never saw the light of day. "On the week that the documentary was supposed to have been featured in *Life,*" Woodruff recalled years later, "Hitler with his army moved into Poland and that buried the feature forever." The disappointment was not a defeat. Woodruff continued to paint and remained an artistic force for decades to come.

Within days of Nazi Germany's invasion of Poland in September 1939, Britain and France declared war on Germany for the start of World War II (1939–1945). Many Americans wanted the United States to remain neutral. That all changed on December 7, 1941, when Germany's ally Japan attacked American naval forces at Hawaii's Pearl Harbor. The next day, President Franklin Roosevelt announced America's entry into the war.

On December 9, though America was still in a state of shock, the exhibit American Negro Art, Nineteenth and Twentieth Centuries, opened at lower

Manhattan's Downtown Gallery. Edith Halpert, who ran the gallery, had planned the exhibition in consultation with Alain Locke. Other white-owned galleries in New York City had planned similar exhibits around that time as part of a small movement to promote black artists. In the wake of Pearl Harbor, the Downtown Gallery was one of the few that did not cancel its exhibitions, which included work by Henry Tanner, Charles Alston, and twenty-five-year-old Jacob Lawrence, a rising star.

The month before this exhibit, the Downtown Gallery had exhibited what became Lawrence's best-known work, the series "The Migration of the Negro." Through sixty paintings of vibrant color and edgy composition, Lawrence captured the traumas and triumphs millions of children and adults experienced during the Great Migration. Also in November 1941, *Fortune* magazine had reproduced twenty-six of the "Migration" paintings, bringing the series to the attention of millions. Art critics quickly hailed "Migration" as a magnificent accomplishment, and Jacob Lawrence, a spectacular talent. It was a talent that had been nurtured in Harlem.

Jacob Lawrence was twelve years old in 1930 when his mother, who believed in the adage "idle hands are the devil's workshop," enrolled him in the arts-and-crafts program at Utopia Children's House. Under the expert eye of his instructor Charles Alston, a graphic artist, sculptor, and painter, young Lawrence reveled in woodworking and making papier-mâché masks.

From almost the minute Lawrence started at Utopia, Alston said he "sensed in him an unusual and unique ability." Alston did all in his power to

JACOB LAWRENCE
(1917–2000)

AND THE MIGRANTS KEPT COMING, PANEL 60
FROM "THE MIGRATION SERIES"
1940–1941
BY JACOB LAWRENCE
TEMPERA ON GESSO ON COMPOSITION BOARD
12 X 18 IN.

In this painting, people crowd a railroad platform, waiting for the train that will take them and their belongings from the South to the northern cities, where they will begin a new life. As many workers joined the military to fight during World War I, there was a new demand for labor in northern cities. At the same time, boll weevil attacks on cotton crops in the South had destroyed harvests, causing many jobs to disappear.

Jacob Lawrence painted "The Migration of the Negro" (later called "The Migration Series") just as America was entering World War II. When Pearl Harbor was bombed, Jacob Lawrence was in New Orleans on a Rosenwald grant that allowed him to keep painting even after the WPA had ended.

Captain Skinner
1944
BY JACOB LAWRENCE
GOUACHE ON PAPERBOARD
29 1/8 X 21 1/8 IN.

When Jacob Lawrence was inducted into the Coast Guard he was assigned to St. Augustine, Florida. Lawrence's superior, Captain J. B. Rosenthal, chose him to serve in the first racially integrated crew in the Coast Guard under the command of Lieutenant Carleton Skinner. Lawrence admired Skinner, and the sentiment was apparently mutual; Skinner had Lawrence rated as a public relations specialist so he could be assigned to draw and paint.

help that ability develop at Utopia and later at his WPA-funded Harlem Art Workshop. Lawrence's talent, particularly for narrative painting, gained strength at Augusta Savage's Harlem Community Art Center. With Alston's help,

Lawrence received a two-year scholarship to the American Artists School in downtown Manhattan.

Charles Seifert was another Harlemite who played an enlightening role in young Lawrence's life. Barbados-born Seifert, who supported himself and his passion for history as a contractor, amassed an impressive collection of manuscripts, books, artwork, and other black-history materials, which were housed in his Ethiopian School of Research on West 137th Street. Seifert was on a mission to share his knowledge with as many people as he could. One way he did this was through his history lectures at the 135th Street library. Lawrence first met Seifert at one of these lectures.

Later, in the spring of 1935, Seifert took Lawrence and several other young Harlemites to see the second, and at that point the largest, exhibition of black African art at a prominent American museum. African Negro Art was held at one of America's first museums devoted to modern art, the Museum of Modern Art (MoMA) in midtown Manhattan. More white Americans were beginning to see the masks, textiles, sculptures, and other black African creations not as curiosities by primitive people, but as intelligent design—as art. "The show made a great impression on me," Lawrence said years later. One result is that it deepened his interest in his heritage.

By 1938, Jacob Lawrence had his drawings and paintings in several group shows, and would have a solo exhibition at the Harlem YMCA on 135th Street. Also in 1938, with Augusta Savage's help, Lawrence secured a job with the WPA Federal Arts Project: an eighteen-month assignment to create two paintings every six weeks. During this time, Lawrence developed an affinity for the serial.

Lawrence's first series, "Toussaint L'Ouverture," was named after the leader of the uprising that led to Haiti's independence. Lawrence's next series of thirty-two paintings honored the abolitionist Frederick Douglass. He made thirty-one paintings on the life of Harriet Tubman. A Rosenwald grant allowed

THE LIBRARY
1960
BY JACOB LAWRENCE
TEMPERA ON
FIBERBOARD
24 X 29 7/8 IN.

By the time Jacob Lawrence painted *The Library* in 1960, he was already one of the most successful black artists of the twentieth century. Lawrence used bold colors and planar, angular forms to create a recognizable—though nearly abstract—composition. The figures hunched over their books are clear. In a couple of open books, Lawrence plainly shows images of African art. In this quiet scene, people seek knowledge of their culture and contributions, just as Lawrence himself did. In the structure of this painting, the bright palette and decisive lines convey strength and determination.

Lawrence to paint "Migration." After "Migration," Lawrence produced more great paintings—including a series on the abolitionist John Brown.

Lawrence was inducted into the U.S. Coast Guard in the fall of 1943. It was not an artistic setback. Though he began as a cook's assistant, his captain soon recognized his talent and gave him other work. He was assigned to paint a chronicle of Coast Guard life. *Captain Skinner, Holystoning the Deck, Signal Practice,* and *Recreation (Boxing)* are among the many paintings from Lawrence's coast guard days.

Some of those paintings, along with "Migration," were included in Lawrence's historic solo exhibition at MoMA in the fall of 1944. Only one other black person—folk artist William Edmondson in 1937—had had a solo show there. By the mid-1940s, Jacob Lawrence was well on his way to becoming one of America's most highly regarded artists.

Like many other artists, Lawrence felt compelled to paint about the war. His "War" series (1946–1947), includes fourteen paintings that portray soldiers on patrol, sailors on leave, and someone stateside in agony after receiving news that a loved one has become a casualty.

Another artist influenced by the war was painter William H. Johnson, who at the time lived in Europe. Had Adolph Hitler never risen to power, Johnson might never have returned to America in the late 1930s, a move that had great impact on his work.

In 1918, at age seventeen, Johnson, who loved to draw as a child, left his hometown of Florence, South Carolina, to study art in New York City. There, Johnson worked as a short-order cook, porter, and dock worker, scrimping and saving until, in 1921, he finally had enough money to enroll in the city's oldest art school, the National Academy of Design. During his years of study at the academy, Johnson won several of the school's prizes. He also found great favor with one of his instructors, the renowned white realist painter Charles

Hawthorne. Hawthorne was determined that Johnson should go to France, and helped him raise money for the trip.

Johnson arrived in France in the winter of 1926. Initially he was attracted to impressionism and then to expressionism, where a subject is not presented exactly as it appears in life, but in a way that captures, or expresses, how an artist thinks or feels about that subject. Like Hale Woodruff, Johnson loved the work of Cézanne and other artists who worked in strong colors, most notably the Frenchman Paul Gauguin and his Dutch friend Vincent van Gogh. But Johnson's idol was the Russian Chaim Soutine, known for his wild brush strokes and fre-

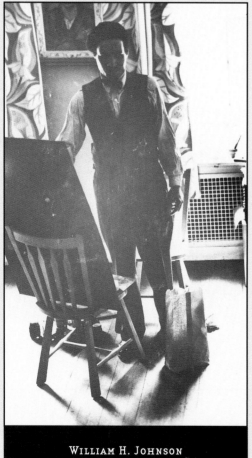

WILLIAM H. JOHNSON
(1901–1970)

netic landscapes. When Johnson discovered that Soutine had created some of his greatest works in Cagnes, a village on the coast of southern France, he decided to live and paint there. But he did not stay there long. During his first few years in Europe, Johnson spent time in the French resort town of Nice and on the island of Corsica. He also visited Belgium and Denmark. Wherever he went, he painted beautiful, emotionally charged landscapes. While in Cagnes, he wrote to his mentor Charles Hawthorne, "I am not afraid to exaggerate a contour, a form, or anything that gives more character and movement to the canvas." While in France, Johnson also sought out Henry Tanner, who very much admired Johnson's work.

At the urging of Palmer Hayden, Johnson returned to America in 1929 to enter several paintings in the upcoming Harmon competition. His decision was a good one. Johnson won the gold medal, and exhibited two portraits, a self-portrait, and

FRUIT TREES AND
MOUNTAINS
ABOUT 1936–1938
BY WILLIAM H.
JOHNSON
OIL ON BURLAP
28 1/2 X 35 1/8 IN.

In works such as *Fruit Trees and Mountains*, William H. Johnson used the bold colors, exaggerated forms, and brisk brush strokes of the German expressionist school. These artists wanted to communicate their feelings about a subject rather than to strictly reproduce its likeness.

*CHILDREN AT
ICE CREAM STAND*
ABOUT 1939–1942
BY WILLIAM H. JOHNSON
TEMPERA AND PEN
AND INK WITH
PENCIL ON PAPER
12 5/8 X 15 IN.

A group of children has gathered around an ice cream vendor to choose cooling treats on a warm summer afternoon. In this apparently casual work on paper, William H. Johnson has used his "primitive" style to create a sophisticated composition. The geometric bodies of the people are layered over the flat, vertical rectangles of the buildings. Johnson created receding, paper-thin layers of depth with the vendors' stands and the rectangular clouds layered above and behind the buildings.

three landscapes at the foundation's annual exhibition. "He is a real modernist," the Harmon judges declared of Johnson. "He has been spontaneous, vigorous, firm and direct."

With these triumphs to spur him on, Johnson returned to Europe, and married a woman he had met earlier in Cagnes, the Danish textile artist Holcha Krake. They married in Denmark and eventually settled in Kerteminde, a fishing village. But the couple was constantly on the move. Throughout the 1930s, they traveled in Europe and North Africa. Along the way, Johnson produced an extraordinary body of work. Whether working in warm colors or hot, he always conveyed the vigor he saw in his subjects, from Tunisian mosques and Norwegian fjords and harbors to Danish farmhouses, mountain streams, seasides, and sunsets. But with the rise of Fascism in Germany and Italy, Europe was changing quickly.

Hitler, at this time chancellor of Germany, hated certain groups of people and certain kinds of art. He thought modern art detestable, in part because of its indebtedness to black African art, which he called "nigger art." Hitler, who had once tried his hand at painting, advocated realistic art that portrayed the greatness of the German nation and advanced his ideas about the superiority of the Aryan race. Beginning in the early 1930s, Hitler had modern art removed from German museums. In 1937, the Nazi party condemned modern art by mounting an exhibition of such work, entitled Degenerate Art.

William and Holcha soon ceased to feel so free in Europe. Johnson knew interracial couples were often not accepted in America, but he felt that he and Holcha would be safer in the United States than in Europe. The couple arrived in late 1938 and settled in Manhattan, where William secured a teaching post at the Harlem Community Art Center. During this time, his painting went through a transformation.

Johnson remained unafraid of exaggerating a form and his paintings still

I BAPTIZE THEE
ABOUT 1940
BY WILLIAM H. JOHNSON
OIL ON BURLAP
38 1/8 X 45 1/2 IN.

When William H. Johnson returned to the United States in 1938, he combined his knowledge of European art and his passion for depicting black life. In 1946, Johnson said, "In all my years of painting, I have had one absorbing and inspiring idea, and have worked towards it with unyielding zeal; to give—in simple and stark form—the story of the Negro as he has existed." In *I Baptize Thee*, Johnson purposely simplified lines and flattened forms. Some people think this style looks like folk art, or works by untrained artists. In reality, Johnson was applying his expert knowledge of color and exaggerated forms in a new and challenging style. In these bold paintings, he distilled a story to its most essential forms and patterns.

exuded vitality, but his compositions became flat, and he often used black out-lines or stark contrasts of color. He called this new style "primitive." Johnson painted blacks in sacred (*I Baptize Thee*) and secular (*Jitterbugs*) scenes. He painted days of jubilee (*Wedding Couple*) and tragedies (*Burned Out*). He por-trayed ordinary people (*Cotton Pickers, Miners, Dockyards*) as well as greats, such as scientist George Washington Carver and educator Nanny Burroughs. Johnson also had a fondness for picturing children in the midst of some delight (*Boys' Sunday Trip, Children at Ice Cream Stand*).

The Bible was another favorite subject, and Johnson was one of the first established artists to paint its characters—from Ezekiel to Jesus—as black. And, like Jacob Lawrence, William Johnson explored his feelings about the war through his art, including works such as *Induction Center, Going to War,* and *Killed in Action.*

More than fifty-five million people died during World War II. The horrors of the war had many intelligent, sensitive souls pondering the meaning of life. Some questioned and abandoned their beliefs and ideals. Others hoped that the catastrophe would give rise to a stronger, international commitment to make the world a better place.

Struggling to express their pain, anger, and hope, many artists turned to extreme abstraction while others explored new realms of realism. European artists who had fled Europe during the war brought new energies and ideas onto the American art scene. Black artists continued to contribute to this diversity—blazing new trails and refashioning ancient traditions.

Jesus Is My Air Plane (detail)
ABOUT 1970
BY SISTER GERTRUDE MORGAN
TEMPERA, BALLPOINT PEN AND INK,
AND PENCIL ON PAPER
18 X 26 3/8 IN.

UPWARD & OUTWARD

America experienced an economic boom after the war. More people could afford to purchase art; they also supported the arts by funding museums, art schools, and art departments. The Servicemen's Readjustment Act, better known as the G.I. Bill, paid returning military personnel to attend college. (During the war, soldiers had picked up the nickname "G.I." for "government issue.") As a result, thousands of men entered every kind of training—including art school. The American art scene, fueled by European immigrants, returning G.I.s, and the prosperity that followed the war, was on fire.

Painter Hughie Lee-Smith worked and thrived in this rich atmosphere. Having served in the Navy, he went to college on the G.I. Bill, and earned a degree in arts education at Michigan's Wayne State University. Lee-Smith had grown up in Cleveland, Ohio, where he "drew all the time. . . . I breathed [art]. I dreamed it. Art was my whole being, and I knew from an early age that it was my mission."

When Lee-Smith graduated from Wayne State in 1953, the prominent art movement was abstract expressionism. Painters such as Willem de Kooning and Jackson Pollock applied their paint to huge canvases, determined to portray pure emotion, usually with little or no concern for representing physical forms. They were obsessed with the quality of the surface they were creating and with the act of painting itself. In contrast, Lee-Smith was committed to filling canvases with recognizable themes and subjects. His dominant theme was alienation: painting after painting of quiet, eerie scenes of people in isolation and perhaps on the edge of despair. Or hope? Many feature young people, some black, some not, often with their backs to the viewer or in profile and shadow. Frequently, their surroundings are bleak and scarred. Lee-Smith's paintings capture an aspect of his emotional autobiography.

HUGHIE LEE-SMITH
(1915–1999)

"In my case, aloneness, I think, has stemmed from the fact that I'm black," Lee-Smith told a journalist in the late 1970s. "[Artists'] work depends upon our being alone, and we can appreciate the condition of aloneness more than other people. Being one of a group of outcasts in a society makes my sensitivity to the condition of aloneness much sharper. . . . I felt it much more in my youth."

Whereas Lee-Smith so often trained his talent on capturing solitude, John Biggers generally focused on the power and blessing of community. "All my things," Biggers once said, "deal with the collective soul of my community. . . . There is so much

THE STRANGER
ABOUT 1957–1958
BY HUGHIE LEE-SMITH
OIL ON CANVAS
26 1/4 X 36 1/8 IN.

When described in words, the elements of this painting—a landscape surrounding a group of sunlit farm buildings, a slight though muscular young man walking under a darkening sky—could be the same as those of a painting by Edward Bannister. But Hughie Lee-Smith's composition makes the viewer uneasy. The buildings are so starkly lit they seem to be isolated from the landscape, and even without the clue given in the title, the man's stance suggests that he does not belong here.

beauty as we walk the razor's edge." This idea is evident in his poignant work *Shotgun, Third Ward #1.*

John Biggers grew up in a tight-knit black enclave in Gastonia, North Carolina. Along with his six siblings, young John (the baby of the family) learned from his parents the life-sustaining principles of self-respect and self-reliance. His father, Paul, who had lost a leg as a boy working in a sawmill, had many talents—farmer, shoemaker, carpenter, school principal, and Baptist preacher. His mother, Cora, was an artist herself—she made beautiful quilts.

John Biggers attended the boarding school where his parents had met, Lincoln Academy in Kings Mountain, North Carolina. Some of his fellow students were Africans. The school's principal, Dr. Henry C. McDowell, had been a missionary in West Africa for twenty years, and he exposed his students to African history and culture.

Though young Biggers had always loved to draw, when he entered Virginia's Hampton Institute (now Hampton University), he planned to be a plumber. That plan was abandoned when he took an art course with Viktor Lowenfeld, the person who started Hampton's art department. Lowenfeld, who was Jewish, had fled his native Austria in the wake of Nazi persecution of his people.

As a member of a persecuted group, Lowenfeld could empathize with blacks in America. He was keenly aware of the toll prejudice can take on young people. He believed self-love was the antidote and he encouraged his students to capture their lives, their history and heritage, in their art. Lowenfeld exposed his students to the work of black Americans (Jacob Lawrence's

JOHN BIGGERS
(1924–2001)

LOIS MAILOU JONES

(1905–1998)

At the time that Boston-born Lois Mailou Jones painted this canvas, she was studying art at the Académie Julian in Paris. There, on the basis of merit, prestigious salons and galleries exhibited her paintings.

The title of this work, *Les Fétiches*, is French for "the fetishes." Fetishes are objects that are believed to have magical powers and are often revered and used in elaborate ceremonies or rituals. Jones's depiction includes African masks floating in space. Bright colors against the black background infuse these images with a sense of their supernatural power. Despite her flat forms, the composition's undulating curves create a sense of electricity and movement.

Jones eventually painted and exhibited all over the world, including Haiti and many countries in Africa. She also influenced generations of American artists in her long career as an art professor at Howard University in Washington, D.C.

LES FÉTICHES
1938
BY LOIS MAILOU JONES
OIL ON LINEN
21 X 25 1/2 IN.

SHOTGUN, THIRD WARD #1
1966
BY JOHN BIGGERS
TEMPERA AND OIL ON CANVAS
30 X 48 IN.

Shotgun houses are commonly found in some areas of the South. One tradition says they are so called because the shot from a shell fired through the front door of the house would pass straight down the hall and out the back door. Here, a community of men and women who have emerged from their houses are gathered on the sidewalk. Those who can bear to look watch their church burn, while others turn away. The children dance on the wet street in the reflected light of the fire.

"Migration" for one) as well as black African art. In Lowenfeld, Biggers found a great mentor and, eventually, a friend.

At Hampton, Biggers also studied with painter, printmaker, and sculptor Elizabeth Catlett and her husband at the time, Charles White. He was acclaimed for highly detailed drawings and paintings. "Charlie White had a tremendous influence on me and my work," Biggers later recalled. Biggers served as White's "apprentice in an informal sense" when White was at work on his mural *The Contribution of the Negro to American Democracy.* "We stood around him in awe, watching this master draftsman . . . model our heroes and ancestors. . . . John Henry, Leadbelly, Shango, and Harriet-the-Moses." Biggers had the thrill of serving as a model for an escapee from slavery in *Contribution*.

Like Charles White, Biggers became a master draftsman. He also earned a doctorate from Pennsylvania State University and founded the art department at Houston's Texas State University for Negroes (renamed Texas Southern University [TSU] in 1951). In those early years at TSU, Biggers and his friend Joseph L. Mack were the entire art faculty, working hard to offer good courses and to attract students. Biggers also made a lot of art, including a mural for the YMCA in Houston's predominantly black Third Ward, *The Contribution of Negro Women to American Life and Education.*

In the early 1950s, Biggers won several prizes, but there were times when a win had a "razor's edge." In the 1952 Dallas Museum of Art competition, Biggers won a prize for *Sleeping Boy,* a tender drawing of a slender child of indeterminate race. On the evening that Biggers came to the museum for the reception planned in his honor, he was handed a check (his prize money) and brusquely informed that the event had been cancelled. When his sculpture *Kneeling Man* won the 1953 Atlanta University annual art show, it was a triumph Biggers could savor—both he and his work were fully accepted.

In the late 1950s, Biggers went to West Africa on a fellowship funded

BEAUFORD DELANEY

(1901–1979)

Beauford Delaney and his younger brother Joseph both began drawing at an early age, and both became artists and gravitated to New York City. There in Greenwich Village, Beauford drew a warm circle of friends around him, including writers, dancers, musicians, and other artists. During the 1930s he worked for the WPA. Though the term would not be invented until the 1950s, some critics call his work from the Depression years abstract impressionism. After World War II, Delaney moved to Paris, where his charm and dedication to art again gained him a group of supporters. His friend the writer James Baldwin said of him, "Perhaps I should not say, flatly, what I believe—that he is a great painter; but I do know that great art can only be created out of love, and that no greater lover ever held a brush."

ABSTRACTION
ABOUT 1955–1965
BY BEAUFORD DELANEY
GOUACHE ON PAPER
22 1/2 X 17 IN.

WAKE UP OUR SOULS

by the United Nations educational and cultural agency UNESCO. He spent a rich six months exploring and painting Ghana, Togo, Nigeria, and Dahomey (as Benin was then known). "I had a magnificent sense of coming home, of belonging," Biggers said of his time in Africa. He was not interested in capturing Africans who had adopted Western ways. Instead, he produced dozens of drawings and paintings of fishermen launching their boats into the sea, women dancing in harvest festivals, and other scenes of people living to the rhythms of homeland and heritage. Biggers published a book of these drawings when he returned to America called *Ananse: The Web of Life in Africa*. The trickster of West African folklore, Anansi the Spider, inspired the title.

When *Ananse* was published in 1962, America was in the midst of shake-up and change. In 1954, in the landmark case *Brown v. Board of Education,* the U.S. Supreme Court outlawed segregation in public schools. After the *Brown* decision, more momentous events compelled streams of people, including non-blacks, to join the civil rights campaign. The 1955–1956 bus boycott in Montgomery, Alabama, protested that city's segregated transportation system; a spate of lunch-counter sit-ins in 1960 condemned "whites-only" service in restaurants; and the Freedom Rides of 1961 called for desegregation of interstate transportation. In 1962, several civil rights organizations began planning what would be the largest demonstration America had yet seen. On August 28, 1963, about 250,000 people assembled for the March on Washington for Jobs and Freedom. Reverend Martin Luther King Jr. stood on the steps of the Lincoln Memorial to deliver his rousing speech-sermon, "I Have a Dream."

A few weeks before that epic event, some artists in New York City came together to discuss their work in the context of the turbulent times. They wrestled with the question of the artist's duty. Should they consciously make art that in some way would aid their people's campaign for equal opportunity? Or should they create art that springs organically, naturally, from their individual

JOSEPH DELANEY

(1904–1991)

Penn Station was the hub of travel to and from New York during World War II. In this painting, businessmen hustle toward their trains or taxis, soldiers say farewell to their sweethearts, and exhausted travelers sink to the floor hoping for a moment's rest. A clock above the crowd reminds them all to hurry, and a flag inspires their patriotic efforts for the war. Joseph Delaney captured the restless energy of that time. He painted many portraits, but he also loved intricate crowd scenes.

Delaney left Tennessee after he completed high school, and went from city to city, taking a variety of jobs. He moved to New York during the Depression and began to study with leading regionalist painter Thomas Hart Benton.

PENN STATION
AT WAR TIME
1943
BY JOSEPH DELANEY
OIL ON CANVAS
34 X 48 1/8 IN.

interests and visions?

This gathering of about a dozen artists included Richard Mayhew (best known for impressionist landscapes), Jacob Lawrence's mentor Charles Alston, abstract expressionist Norman Lewis, and Hale Woodruff, who had been teaching art at New York University since the mid-1940s. This gathering became a group that would meet twice a month to talk about their work and a range of issues. Hale Woodruff suggested the group's name: Spiral, a symbol of positive motion—upward and outward.

Although the issue of the artist's duty remained a subject of debate, Spiral eventually agreed to mount an exhibition, with the proceeds to go to a civil rights organization. The show opened in the spring of 1965 and was entitled Works in Black and White, to symbolize racial tension. Each artist contributed a work in only those two colors. Romare Bearden, in whose Canal Street studio Spiral first met, was the driving force behind Works in Black and White.

Romare Bearden—"Romie" to family and friends—was born in Charlotte, North Carolina. When he was very young, his politically active parents moved to Harlem. W. E. B. Du Bois, Langston Hughes, jazz master Duke Ellington, and Romie's cousin Charles Alston were among the activists and artists who visited the Bearden home. Another was Aaron Douglas, best known for murals and illustrations that used motifs from Egyptian art.

During his teens, Bearden spent stretches of time in Pittsburgh, Pennsylvania, with his maternal

ROMARE BEARDEN
(1912–1988)

SPRING WAY
1964
BY ROMARE BEARDEN
COLLAGE
ON PAPERBOARD
6 5/8 X 9 3/8 IN.

Spring Way relies almost completely on architectural geometric forms in a range of blacks and grays; the insertions of vivid red add intensity and emphasize the sense of space. Romare Bearden's means and media were constantly evolving; he sometimes cut up one of his paintings and incorporated the pieces into collages, but he considered it all part of the same process. He said in 1970, "I paint on collages. I consider them paintings, not collage."

grandmother, Carrie. During one Pittsburgh summer, he struck up a friendship with a sickly boy named Eugene, who made art on brown paper bags. "He did these marvelous drawings of houses with no fronts on them," Bearden recalled years later. "You could see everything that was going on in all the rooms." When Bearden asked Eugene to teach him to draw, Eugene did. This friendship was short-lived as Eugene died shortly thereafter.

Bearden first attended Lincoln University in Pennsylvania, then Boston University, where he took drawing classes and contributed cartoons to the student magazine, *The Beanpot*. Finally, he transferred to New York University, where he took more art classes, became editor of the university's humor magazine, *Medley*, and earned a bachelor's degree in education (1935).

During the 1930s, Bearden, whose love for jazz was equal to his love for visual art, became friends with a range of New York artists, from Augusta Savage and Jacob Lawrence to leading white abstract painters, including Robert Motherwell, Carl Holty, and Stuart Davis. In 1936, Bearden enrolled in the Art Students League in downtown Manhattan. There, he studied with the German painter George Grosz, one of the major forces of expressionism. Some of Bearden's work (much of it paintings of life in Harlem) was shown in group exhibitions, including American Negro Art, Nineteenth and Twentieth Centuries, in 1941.

By the time Spiral formed in the early 1960s, Bearden was on the verge of something new. He had stopped painting altogether for a time and dabbled in songwriting. (One of his songs, "Seabreeze," became a hit!) Bearden had fallen in love with abstract expressionism and then found that semi-abstraction appealed to him more. And Bearden had long since chosen his "artist gods." They included Picasso and Henri Matisse, leader of the early twentieth-century movement fauvism (after the French word for "wild beast"), with its use of bold, festive colors and distortion of shapes. Black

NORMAN LEWIS

(1909–1979)

A lyrical tracery of lines, a shimmering of red, white, and blue brush strokes dance across the canvas in *Evening Rendezvous*. On closer examination, a procession of standing and mounted figures wearing white robes and hoods emerges, perhaps burning crosses or brandishing torches. The artist is showing a secret meeting of the Ku Klux Klan in the dead of night. The red, white, and blue colors, synonymous with America, assume sinister overtones. When Norman Lewis painted this work during the 1960s, the Ku Klux Klan was responding to the Civil Rights movement by organizing violent attacks against civil rights workers in cities throughout the South.

A lifelong advocate of social justice,

Lewis, who was born in Harlem, began his career during the 1930s as a realist painter and later turned to nonrepresentational art. He demonstrated his solidarity with the civil rights movement with a series of powerful abstractions. He is considered the first major black abstract expressionist.

EVENING RENDEZVOUS
1962
BY NORMAN LEWIS
OIL ON LINEN
50 1/4 X 64 1/4 IN.

EMPRESS OF THE BLUES
1974
BY ROMARE BEARDEN
ACRYLIC AND PENCIL ON
PRINTED PAPER ON PAPERBOARD
36 X 48 IN.

An exuberant Bessie Smith, the "Empress of the Blues," sings in the collage, as does its maker, Romare Bearden, through his rhythmic arrangements of form and color. Bearden thought of collage as a visual equivalent of music. To produce his collage, he assembled sharply angled pieces of colored paper and magazine pages. Bessie Smith was one of the many blues performers Bearden saw at the Lafayette Theatre when he was growing up in Harlem during the late 1920s. Backing up the spellbinding soloist is a full band, including a pianist, drummer, bass player, jazz guitarist, trumpeters, saxophonists, trombonists, and clarinetists. The background, a bold geometry of red, green, and blue, underscores the pulsing music.

African art was also a guiding light, and Bearden studied calligraphy and Chinese landscape painting with a Chinese man who ran a bookshop not far from Bearden's Canal Street studio. In the summer of 1963, Bearden was about to find himself as an artist.

During Spiral's initial discussions of Works in Black and White, Bearden had proposed a huge collaborative collage. When the group expressed no interest in the idea, Bearden pressed on with it alone. He transformed images he cut out of magazines into collages about the places that shaped his boyhood: Charlotte, Pittsburgh, and Harlem. Bearden enlarged the works and affixed them to Masonite. His interest in the project waned until the day Arne Ekstrom, co-owner of the Manhattan gallery where Bearden showed his work, spotted the collages at Bearden's studio. Ekstrom urged him to make those collages his next show.

They titled the show Projections. When the show opened at Cordier & Ekstrom gallery in the fall of 1964 it was a huge success. A year later, Projections was on view at Washington, D.C.'s prestigious Corcoran Gallery of Art.

Bearden had found his greatest gift. He went on to distinguish himself at collage, largely projecting, as he put it, "the life of my people as I know it." Bearden knew the enormous ingenuity many blacks summoned up to survive. In his art he captured this "making a way out of no way," which he also saw in spirituals, the blues, and jazz. Whether his central figures are grooving on a bandstand or living in a shack, they convey the thing that so impressed his friend Hale Woodruff about black African art: "a very great sense of self."

While Bearden became a master collagist, one of his friends and frequent jazz club comrades, Roy DeCarava, became a master photographer. But as a boy delighting in his sidewalk chalk drawings, DeCarava had no idea that photography would later be his life's work.

When Roy DeCarava graduated from New York City's Textile High School, he

FELRATH HINES

(1913–1993)

Felrath Hines is best known for his elegant abstract paintings of radiant colors and subtle compositions. In *Yellow and Gray* the warmth of the yellows contrasts with the coolness of the various grays. The circles and elongated forms could be seen as a fierce summer sun breaking through an overcast sky, but Hines was more interested in simplifying shapes and colors than in depicting a landscape. In the painting, Hines explores how colors change when placed against each other. For instance, the medium gray horizontal band looks darker to the left of the circle than to the right, though in truth they are the same. His pure colors and forms speak of mystery and wholeness.

Born in Indianapolis, Indiana, Hines was a prominent member of the artists' collective Spiral. In addition to art, Hines studied art conservation and made his living for many years restoring artworks for museums in New York and Washington, D.C.

YELLOW AND GRAY
1976
BY FELRATH HINES
OIL ON LINEN
54 1/4 X 48 IN.

was intent on being a painter. He pursued that goal through two years of study at the Cooper Union, and additional training at the Harlem Community Art Center and Harlem's George Washington Carver Art School, where he studied with one of John Biggers's mentors, Charles White.

Like other painters, DeCarava took photographs of people, places, and things as reference material for his paintings. The more he shot, the more interested he became in the medium. In the late 1940s, he decided to make photography his primary art. "Through the camera I was able to make contact with the world," he later explained, "and express my feelings about it more directly." One of the things he wanted to express was his love for black people and his impressions of their strengths and beauty.

In 1950, DeCarava had a solo exhibition at a midtown Manhattan gallery of a white friend, Mark Perper. The white photographer Homer Page, who helped with the display of the photographs, encouraged DeCarava to show some of his work to Edward Steichen, head of MoMA's photography department. Steichen purchased some of DeCarava's photographs and encouraged him to apply for a fellowship from New York City's Guggenheim Foundation. At first DeCarava sloughed off the idea, but he eventually applied. Much to his astonishment, in 1952 he became the ninth photographer and the first black photographer to receive a Guggenheim fellowship. The grant allowed DeCarava to devote a year to photography. Understandably, DeCarava thought that news of his fellowship would result in more interest in his work. Though disheartened when that did not occur, he continued to take picture after picture.

ROY DECARAVA
(1919–PRESENT)

GRADUATION, NEW YORK
1949, PRINTED 1982
BY ROY DECARAVA
GELATIN SILVER PRINT
ON PAPER
10 7/8 X 14 IN.

This is one of the 140 photographs Roy DeCarava included in his collaboration with Langston Hughes, *The Sweet Flypaper of Life*. Here, the pristine white of the girl's dress shines against the gritty backdrop of brick and concrete. As the shiny new car on the poster drives off the edge of the image to a more prosperous future, will it leave this hopeful Cinderella behind?

DeCarava thought his big chance had arrived when MoMA included some of his photographs in its landmark exhibition, The Family of Man: roughly five hundred photographs revealing the ties that bind people of various cultures

FORT SCOTT, KANSAS
1950
BY GORDON PARKS
GELATIN SILVER PRINT ON PAPER
13 1/2 X 9 1/2 IN.

GORDON PARKS

(1912–PRESENT)

Gordon Parks grew up in Fort Scott, Kansas. He was the youngest of fifteen children, and he knew both poverty and racism firsthand. In his 1963 autobiographical novel, *The Learning Tree,* he describes his desperation to escape that life. But he never quit using the experiences of his childhood. Over the years, he returned to his hometown again and again to photograph its familiar people and places. It is easy to imagine Parks's sympathy with this man, isolated and wrapped in his own thoughts. But the crisp focus of the figure against the blurred background and the light caressing his face and hands suggest that he will find a way to realize his desires and dreams.

around the world. As with the Guggenheim fellowship, after the Family of Man opened in 1955, DeCarava received no major press. No museum curators or gallery owners clamored to exhibit his work. "So I had 500 or 600 pictures sitting up in my closet, and no place to show them." DeCarava had had exhibits in two public libraries (one in Harlem; the other in Greenwich Village) but those shows had not made a splash. "After that it was just quiet."

Instead of giving up, in that same year DeCarava decided to exhibit his work himself. He and his wife, Sherry, transformed part of their apartment on West 84th Street into a gallery. They named it simply "A Photographer's Gallery," and DeCarava showed the work of other photographers along with his own.

In 1955, DeCarava published his book *The Sweet Flypaper of Life,* containing more than one hundred photographs of joys and sorrows of everyday folks in Harlem, with text by Langston Hughes. The book was a result of DeCarava's resourcefulness. He had contacted Hughes, whose writing career included a column for the *New York Post*. Hughes had been, as DeCarava put it, "a familiar presence" at the Harlem Community Art Center. DeCarava hoped Hughes could help his work get some publicity, "Why don't you do a book?" the writer inquired after looking through DeCarava's photographs. Hughes took the suggestion to one of his publishers and sold them on the idea.

The Sweet Flypaper of Life sold briskly, and the world was no longer quiet about the artistry of Roy DeCarava—about his poignant portraits of Harlem; about his moody portraits of jazz musicians; about his great gift for seeing beauty in the mundane, as revealed in photographs such as *Coathanger and Catsup Bottles,* and *Table and Coat.*

As his stature as a photographer grew, Roy DeCarava helped other black photographers advance. He was cofounder and first president of Kamoinge Workshop, formed in 1963, the same year as Bearden's Spiral. "Kamoinge" means "a group of people acting together" in Kikuyu, an East African language.

The photographers chose the name, as founding member Louis Draper explained, "because it signified a possible way out of the photographic isolation we each felt, individually. . . . This sense of isolation and the general unwelcomeness from downtown magazines and exhibition outlets, served to fuel our collective frustrations. What we needed most was critical feedback and encouragement, the urgency of which was propelled by and ran parallel to human rights struggles exploding upon the national stage."

One of those struggles was for change in the status of women in America. Waves of women (and some men) were pressing for women to receive equal employment opportunity, equal pay for equal work, and for colleges to offer women's studies, among other things. Because of the more militant women's movement of the 1960s and 1970s, more women artists (past and present) came into view and prominence.

ALMA THOMAS
(1891–1978)

Painter Alma Thomas was in that number, receiving major acclaim when she was in her seventies. However, this is hardly a misfortune: she did not begin painting in earnest until she was in her late sixties! But art had always been a major part of her life.

This native of Columbus, Georgia, was born with a hearing impairment and developed a speech impediment, but she allowed neither obstacle to keep her from her zest for life. Alma and her three younger sisters spent many summers at their maternal grandfather's cotton plantation in Alabama—"I remember the gorgeous sunsets; I remember the lovely fowl, every kind of fowl." She also remembered front-porch afternoons watching peacocks "put on their display for us." The plantation's "most

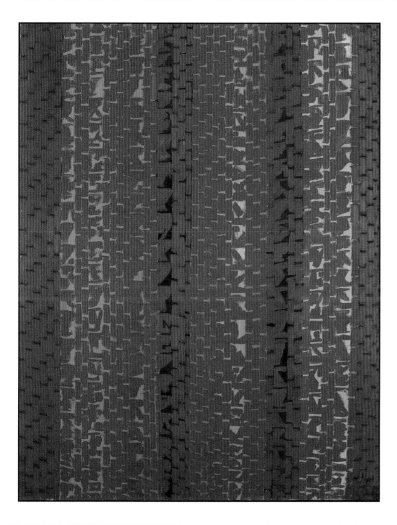

RED SUNSET,
OLD POND CONCERTO
1972
BY ALMA THOMAS
ACRYLIC ON CANVAS
68 1/2 X 52 1/4 IN.

Alma Thomas liked to quote the artist Johannes Itten: "Color is life; for a world without color appears to us as dead. Colors are primordial ideas, the children of light." Though Thomas gave her paintings titles that sounded realistic, her paintings are about the pure joy of manipulating color in a completely abstract manner. She achieved both precision and freedom in her work despite chronic and nearly crippling arthritis in her hands.

unusual wildflowers" utterly amazed young Alma.

When the Thomas family relocated to Washington, D.C., Alma enrolled in Armstrong Technical High School. "When I entered the art room, it was like entering heaven." Thomas took every art course the school offered and after high school she taught arts and crafts at a center for the poor in Wilmington,

Delaware. She went on to major in education at Howard University—but Alma Thomas had no plan to be a career artist. After she graduated from college in the mid-1920s, she embarked on what would be a distinguished career as an art teacher at Washington, D.C.'s Shaw Junior High School. Along the way, Thomas earned a master's degree in education from Teacher's College, Columbia University, and in the 1950s she took art courses at D.C.'s American University, where she became quite intrigued with abstract art.

When Thomas retired from teaching in 1960, she spent more and more of her time painting, with her kitchen doubling as her studio. Then, in 1964, arthritis attacked. "This is the end," she thought. "I'll never be able to move my arms again, or walk."

Arthritis did not have the victory. When James Porter, head of Howard's art department and art gallery, contacted Thomas in 1966 about his desire to have an exhibition of her paintings, Thomas was able and eager to generate new work for the show. She found her inspiration right outside her living room window: in the movement of her holly tree's leaves, in the frolic of light and shadow. This type of painting became Thomas's signature style, perhaps inspired by those early days spent in Alabama. It consists of large canvases of exuberant, multicolored mosaics. These abstractions were inspired by nature, based on Thomas's holly tree, her flower gardens, D.C.'s famous cherry blossoms, or Thomas's frequent visits to the National Arboretum.

Rave reviews led to more shows. The most historic one was a solo show in 1972 at New York City's Whitney Museum of American Art, a leading repository of twentieth-century American art. Thomas was the first black woman to have a solo show at the Whitney since it opened in 1931.

"When I was a little girl, one of the things [blacks in Columbus, Georgia,] couldn't do was go into museums, let alone think of hanging our pictures there," Thomas told a reporter around the time of her Whitney show.

She added, "My, times have changed."

Another change in the late-twentieth-century art world was greater interest in the work of people called "folk artists," "self-taught artists," "naïve artists," "intuitive artists," or "outsider artists." Their art styles and mediums are diverse, but what defines this group is that they have never studied art with an instructor or at an institution that the art establishment recognizes.

One such artist was Sister Gertrude Morgan, a native of LaFayette, Alabama, who moved to New Orleans, Louisiana, when she was in her thirties. In New Orleans, Morgan became a Pentecostal street preacher, singer, song-writer, and musician. For a time, along with two other women, Morgan ran a shelter for orphans, runaways, and other needy children. After Hurricane Betsy wrecked their institution in 1965, Morgan became a home-aide to an elderly woman.

Sister Gertrude Morgan had been making art for several years, giving form and color to her prayer and revelations. With ink, a mix of cheap paints, and crayons, Morgan made art on any and every kind of "canvas" at hand—

scraps of wood, cardboard, lampshades, shower curtains—even her guitar case. Her art is always about repentance. Her paintings urged fellow believers to live sanctified lives and nonbelievers to embrace her source of joy and liberation: Jesus Christ. One of her songs began with the following lines:

Time to wake up and learn about Jesus.
Let us wake and make time to love him.
We have to wake up our souls.

SISTER GERTRUDE MORGAN
(1900-1980)

JESUS IS MY AIR PLANE
ABOUT 1970
BY SISTER GERTRUDE MORGAN
TEMPERA, BALLPOINT PEN AND INK,
AND PENCIL ON PAPER
18 X 26 3/8 IN.

Sister Gertrude Morgan often said that her pictures were composed by God, even though they were drawn by her hands. Her art often interprets parts of the Bible's Book of Revelation or takes the form of a visual sermon.

The Throne of the Third Heaven of the Nations' Millennium General Assembly
ABOUT 1950-1964
BY JAMES HAMPTON
GOLD AND SILVER
ALUMINUM FOIL,
KRAFT PAPER, AND
PLASTIC OVER WOOD
FURNITURE, PAPER-
BOARD, AND GLASS
(180 PIECES IN OVERALL
CONFIGURATION)
10 1/2 X 27 X
14 1/2 FT.

After completing his janitorial duties around midnight, James Hampton worked on *The Throne* for five or six hours almost every night for nearly fifteen years in his rented garage in Washington, D.C. It is an astonishing vision—perhaps his view of heaven—which he fashioned from objects scavenged from sidewalks, dumpsters, and secondhand stores, a heaven made out of a recycled earth. He wrapped in shimmering foil the most ordinary objects, such as discarded light bulbs, and transformed them into a lyrical portrayal of God as the light of the world.

The Throne reflects Hampton's close reading of the Bible's Book of Revelation, which concentrates on the Second Coming of Christ. At this event, as revealed to the prophet John, God appears on a magnificent throne, surrounded by radiant angels. A throne chair is the centerpiece of Hampton's layout. His principal decorative motif—a saw-toothed winged form—suggests angels. Hampton's labels for parts of *The Throne* indicate that those to the left of the throne chair refer to the New Testament, Jesus, and Grace, and those to the right refer to the Old Testament, Moses, and the Law. The symmetrical grouping is capped by the biblical command, "Fear Not."

The only known work by another folk artist, James Hampton, is also a monument to Jesus. Hampton gave his creation a rather long title: *The Throne of the Third Heaven of the Nations' Millennium General Assembly*. Hampton created *The Throne* in a city abounding in monuments, Washington, D.C.

James Hampton, born in the small South Carolina town of Elloree, moved to D.C. in the late 1920s. He worked as a short-order cook and, following a stint in the army, as a janitor for the federal government.

Hardly any of Hampton's workmates and neighbors knew that for years, in a garage he rented in a northwest D.C. alley, this quiet, simple-living man devoted almost the whole of his free time to constructing *The Throne:* a ten-foot-tall assemblage of 180 items, most fashioned from used furniture, variously shaped pieces of cardboard, and discards from other peoples' lives. Hampton covered most of *The Throne* with different kinds of gold- and silver-toned foil.

The work has bedazzled and bewildered countless beholders since its existence became news in the fall of 1964, shortly after Hampton's death. "[*The Throne*] may well be the finest work of visionary religious art produced by an American," one art critic declared.

JAMES HAMPTON
(1909-1964)

"I turned and, beyond the entrance, saw a room filled with light—glimmering, shimmering light reflecting off gold and silver forms," wrote Betye Saar, remembering the first time she saw James Hampton's *The Throne,* at the Whitney Museum in the mid-1970s.

"The room beckoned me," Saar continued. "As I entered the room, I felt a rush from sensory overload. My heartbeat increased, and I felt light-headed and giddy. My eyes couldn't focus. They darted around the room at the many unusual shapes—tables, chairs, and pedestals transformed into dazzling altars of gold and silver." Saar could definitely relate to Hampton's creative process: much of her own artwork is composed of found things, but unlike Hampton, Saar is not a folk artist. She had years of art training.

Collecting odd things was something Saar did as a child in Pasadena, California, the youngest of her parents' three girls. "I'd go out in the back-yard," she remembered, "and find bits of glass and stones in the dirt." When at the beach, she hunted for seashells. Her childhood interest remained with her throughout her years of studying art.

By the mid-1950s, Saar had earned a bachelor's degree from the University of California at Los Angeles, and had embarked on a career as a costume design-er and graphic artist. She went on to attend California State University at Long Beach with the intention of getting a teaching cer-tificate. When printmaking caught her imagination, she changed course, and began work on a master's of fine arts.

BETYE SAAR
(1926–PRESENT)

"A curiosity about the mystical," Saar says, is the thread that runs through all her work. This curiosity is rooted in her memories of being psychic as a child, an ability she has said she lost at age six shortly after her father died. Saar's body of work includes prints incorporating zodiac signs. She also has created tabletop and hanging boxes on and in which she assembled all sorts of found objects, some associated with the occult. Saar's beloved great-aunt Hattie, who died in 1975 at age ninety-eight, inspired one series of boxes. A pincushion, handker-chiefs, jewelry, photographs, and even an egg timer

WISHING FOR WINTER
1989
BY BETYE SAAR
MIXED MEDIA
40 3/4 X 19 1/4 X 2 1/4 IN.

Betye Saar says that she does not go in
search of particular objects to tell a
story, but lets them come to her. This
wooden window frame encases gloves,
feathers, keys, a book, and myriad but-
terfly wings. Each object carries its own
history, but their cumulative meaning
is mysterious.

are among the artifacts of that great-aunt's life that Saar transformed into a work of art. Saar has also created altars that echo age-old traditions and ceremonies out of Haiti, Mexico, and various African nations.

In the late twentieth century, Saar was far from the only artist creating mixed-media art. A multitude of artists explored all kinds of concepts and materials. The possibilities for art seemed limitless. Renée Stout is another artist who staked a claim in art's new frontiers. Pebbles from West Africa, roots and herbs, beads, dolls, and a thrown-away bench are among the mementos and "junk" Renée Stout has used in her sculptures.

Stout was born in Junction City, Kansas, and spent most of her youth in Pittsburgh, Pennsylvania. Her mother was a superb seamstress; her father, something of a mechanical genius. Stout also had a grandfather whose hobbies included carving toys for her and other children, and her mother's brother Jesse had a passion for painting. As a child, Stout found release for some of her creative energies in Saturday art classes at the Carnegie Museum.

RENÉE STOUT
(1958–PRESENT)

When Stout decided to be an artist, she had no plans to be a sculptor. Instead, after she earned a bachelor's degree from Pittsburgh's Carnegie-Mellon University in 1980, she was committed to being a painter. Stout's transformation as an artist began in 1984, during her residency at Northeastern University in Boston, Massachusetts.

Stout and Boston were not a good fit. She never felt at home there, and became something of a loner. Solitude led to introspection, to "looking inward and looking more into myself," as she put it. She continued looking within when she moved to Washington, D.C., in 1985.

THE COLONEL'S CABINET
1991–1994
BY RENÉE STOUT
MIXED MEDIA
67 1/2 X 60 X
50 1/2 IN.

Renée Stout has created a series of characters based on people she knows or knew. Colonel Frank, the fictitious character of this work's title, is a world traveler who has sent home souvenirs of his travels to his friend Dorothy. She has arranged these artifacts into a kind of shrine, which is also an image of her absent companion. (The Colonel's artifacts actually belonged to a friend's deceased uncle.)

Introspection sent Stout rummaging through childhood memories. She recalled centuries-old artifacts from various cultures she had seen at the Carnegie Museum of Natural History. Especially spellbinding was an *nkisi* figure from West Africa. An *nkisi,* the plural of which is *minkisi,* is a creation of the BaKongo people of present-day Congo and Angola. *Minkisi* are ritual objects believed to have the power to hurt or heal, curse or bless. Usually they are wooden, human figures to which their makers affix (solely or in combination) pieces of cloth, furs, feathers, cowrie shells, stones, bits of glass, and other material with symbolic meaning. Many *minkisi,* like the one Stout saw as a child, are studded with nails.

Stout's memory of that *nkisi* inspired her to create her "Fetish" series, three sculptures echoing *minkisi* compositions. Stout would allow other memories, sharp and fuzzy alike, to serve as the starting points for numerous other artwork

WINNIE OWENS-HART
(1949-PRESENT)

in her quest to "create art that helps me put together what are only fragments, to try to create a whole, so that I can gain a better understanding of my own existence." While admitting that her work is a journey of self-discovery, Stout welcomes others to come along. "In doing this, I hope that others, no matter where they come from, will realize some answers about their own existence."

Things ancient also called to Winnie Owens-Hart, a native of Washington, D.C., where as a child she relished trips to the Museum of Natural History, the National Gallery of Art, and the Museum of African Art, then located in the Frederick Douglass home.

She earned a bachelor's of fine arts in 1971 from Philadelphia College of Art (today the University

Drum with Reptile Motif
1993
by Winnie Owens-Hart
fired earthenware
10 x 11 x 10 in.

This unusual drum is made of clay and is shaped like a jar with an open hole in the side. The drummer plays it by slapping the holes with the palms of the hands and tapping the vessel and the edges of the openings with the fingers. A skilled drummer can produce a wide variety of tones and pitches. During the late 1970s, Winnie Owens-Hart traveled to Nigeria, where she learned local pottery techniques from the women in the village of Ipetumodu. While drumming ceremonies are very important in Nigeria, historically women may play only these ceramic drums, which they make themselves.

of the Arts) and in 1974, a master's of fine arts in ceramics and sculpture at Howard University. Owens-Hart went on to seek out opportunities to broaden her knowledge of pottery. Her search resulted in spending the summer of 1974 at Haystack Mountain School of Crafts in Deer Isle, Maine. Years later, she spent a summer at California's Idyllwild School of Music and the Arts (today Idyllwild Arts

Academy). There, she studied the pottery-making techniques of Pueblo peoples with Blue Corn, one of the most highly acclaimed Native American ceramicists.

Through pottery, Owens-Hart came in closer touch with her own heritage. "African Americans, for a variety of reasons, have been separated from their African heritage for hundreds of years," she noted in an essay. "Many African Americans have sought to reestablish connection—an effort that has taken many forms, from reading books to making pilgrimages [to Africa]. Mine was a journey to the pottery village of Ipetumodu, Nigeria." At Haystack she had studied with the Nigerian artist Abbas Ahuwan. But her time spent in Ipetumodu was the giant step in her "journey toward a more accurate account of the contributions of African ceramicists to the history of world ceramics."

Ipetumodu is an all-female pottery *ebu* ("workshop" in Yoruba) that produces water pots and other vessels for surrounding communities. Winnie Owens-Hart first visited Ipetumodu in the summer of 1977 as a delegate for the second FESTAC (Festival of Arts and Culture), an international conference on art by black people. Two years later, she spent a year in Ipetumodu, apprenticing with a master potter.

"The making of a vessel is one of the oldest forms of art," Owens-Hart pointed out in a statement that accompanied an exhibition of her work in the late 1990s. "The making of that vessel out of clay can be traced back to woman's earliest contributions to civilizations . . . in fact it has been the ceramic object that has informed archaeologists and anthropologists about the inhabitants and lifestyles of those civilizations."

Into the twenty-first century, Winnie Owens-Hart and thousands of other black artists around America continued to inform the world of their feelings, ideas, and memories. Like artists before them, they were committed to moving upward and outward, enlarging the universe of art.

EARLIE HUDNALL JR.

(1946–PRESENT)

Earlie Hudnall Jr. has captured a woman in hat and pearls. Has she come from a luncheon where she was honored, or has she just attended church? She looks as eternal and unmoving as the stone steps behind her. The black tones in the photograph—from the feathers to her blouse and suit jacket—display remarkable depth and richness.

Hudnall was inspired by his father, an amateur photographer, and also his grandmother, who kept a photo album of family members and people in the community. She passed along to her grandson the importance of keeping a visual record. Born in Hattiesburg, Mississippi, Hudnall was a student of John Biggers at Texas State University and has lived for many years in Houston, Texas.

LADY IN BLACK HAT WITH FEATHERS
1990
BY EARLIE HUDNALL JR.
GELATIN SILVER PRINT ON PAPER
19 7/8 X 16 IN.

FAITH RINGGOLD
(1930–PRESENT)

"The Bitter Nest" is a series of five story-quilts that are based on Faith Ringgold's relationships with her two daughters. Ringgold originally created the story as a performance piece; she has called her stories and characters "fantasized adaptation of real life." Eventually, she painted elements of the story on pieces of fabric that she stitched together into the quilts. Daughter Celia and her mother, Cee Cee, are the principal characters in this fictional drama of family differences, set in Harlem during the 1920s. The scene is a dinner party with guests, including painter Aaron Douglas, scholar W. E. B. Du Bois, and writers Richard Wright, Countee Cullen, Zora Neale Hurston, and Langston Hughes. The daughter is mortified as her exotically dressed mother dances to entertain the prominent guests.

Ringgold is best known for her quilts that combine painting, quilted fabric, and storytelling. For her format she was inspired by Tibetan *tankas*, painted religious hangings. Ringgold grew up in Harlem, the daughter of a fashion designer and a sanitation worker.

THE BITTER NEST, PART II:
THE HARLEM RENAISSANCE PARTY
1988
BY FAITH RINGGOLD
ACRYLIC ON CANVAS WITH PRINTED,
DYED, AND PIECED FABRIC
94 X 83 IN.

MELVIN EDWARDS
(1937–PRESENT)

This welded steel sculpture combines a spearhead and a shovel, two iron rods used in soldering, two kinds of wrenches, a portion of an I-beam, a ball-shaped object, and a chain attached to a tire iron. The work is beautiful in its strength, its various textures, and its soaring diagonals. It is named for Oliver Tambo, who died in 1993. Tambo and Nelson Mandela, both anti-apartheid leaders in South Africa, founded the Youth League of the African National Congress (ANC) in 1944. In 1962, Mandela was arrested for attempting to leave South Africa illegally and for inciting a strike. He remained in prison until 1990, and during that time Tambo served as leader of the Youth League.

What accounts for this unusual assemblage of objects? Why is Melvin Edwards welding together a pre-industrial

spear, a tire iron, chains, and tools? The wrenches and girder suggest building and commerce, the shovel, agriculture. The ball and shackle recall the legacy of slavery and injustice, but the spear reminds us of the spirit of resistance. Edwards fuses elements of struggle and aspiration with symbols of urban and rural enterprise.

TAMBO
1993
WELDED STEEL
28 1/8 X 25 1/4
X 22 IN.

AFTERWORD

Centuries from now, when your descendants look back on art in America's first few hundred years, they will see that the story of black artists is the story of a people: a people others once deemed unworthy of freedom; a people who year after decade after century continuously declared their humanity and the validity of their point of view. Art was part of that declaration.

Your descendants will glimpse Joshua Johnson, who spent his early life in captivity. They will see Edward Bannister, treated so shabbily when he inquired about his award-winning painting, "No. 54." They will see Henry Tanner feeling safer, freer in France. And see still others, such as Augusta Savage and Hale Woodruff, keeping America as home and creating institutions so that a Jacob Lawrence or a Roy DeCarava could be. And they will hear Alma Thomas saying, "My, times have changed."

If they are wise—eyes open, hearts alive—your descendants will see more than hardship and struggle, and the overcoming that is certainly worthy of praise. They will see the art—African-infused, European- and other-culture-influenced energies—transforming clay and marble and metal and "junk," and watercolors and oils, and cutouts for collage into fascinating memories and visions. And mysteries. They will see the opportunity art offers people of different cultures to connect with each other. And they will see that, like other artists around the world and throughout the ages, black American artists have created a wealth of visual expression that wakes up our souls to the power of art to help us gain insights into ourselves and our world.

GLOSSARY OF ART TERMS

abstract art: art that does not offer a realistic depiction of an object or scene, but rather offers lines, forms, and colors as the direct expression of ideas or emotions. (*see also* non-objective art)

art conservation: a process in which artworks are treated to prevent or reverse deterioration and damage; good conservators use materials that are distinct from and cause no additional damage to the original.

assemblage: sculpture made up of fragments of natural or manufactured materials such as wood, metal, fabric, and preexisting objects. The word was first used to describe collage, but was soon extended to include sculpture as well. (*see also* mixed media)

background: the part of a painting that seems farthest from the viewer as opposed to the foreground (the area that seems closest to the viewer).

bust: a sculpture or painting of a person's upper body, usually head and shoulders.

canvas: a) the stretched and coated fabric on which an artist paints a picture. Artists' canvas can be made from cotton, flax, hemp, or jute. b) a finished oil painting on a fabric support.

casein: a protein that comes from milk, used as a binding agent (it binds with and carries the pigment or color) for certain kinds of paint.

ceramicist: someone who works with clay.

collage: an artwork made by applying paper and other materials to a flat surface such as a canvas or panel to form a composition; the technique of creating a collage. The practice of collage increased during the early twentieth century in part because so much colorful printed material was newly and easily available. The cubists were among the first to make frequent use of collage.

color: artists consider color for its hue or tint, its shade or intensity, and its effect in relation to other colors. In color theory, the primary hues are red, yellow, and blue, with all other colors (known as secondary and tertiary) being some combination of those three, sometimes with the addition of black or white. In reality, painters often use pigments that are made from natural sources (stone, wood, or even exoskeletons of beetles) that are not the "pure" colors of color theory. Once these are prepared and blended into their medium (such as oil), artists mix them to achieve the colors they want. Some painters favor a particular group of colors, and sometimes talk about that group of colors as their "palette." Blues and greens are often called "cool" colors, while yellows and reds are called "warm" colors. "Hot color" generally uses a large proportion of red, and can also be the result of painting over a base layer of red paint.

commission: an arrangement in which a patron hires an artist to produce a specific work of art, often for a particular place or purpose.

composition: the arrangement of lines, forms, and colors in a work of art.

cubism: a revolution in painting style advanced by Georges Braque and Pablo Picasso between 1909 and 1914 and later adopted by a broadly international group of painters. Cubist painters showed subjects from many viewpoints in the same image so that several aspects of the subject could be shown simultaneously.

curator: a person, often within a museum, whose job includes organizing exhibitions, studying and understanding the works in the museum's collection, and acquiring new artworks for the museum.

detail: a section or part of a work of art; not the whole.

fauvism: a movement in painting known for landscapes painted in intense, non-naturalistic colors. The fauves worked in Paris from 1905 through 1907; Matisse was at the center of the group. The name is French for savage or wild beast.

fine art: usually refers to painting, sculpture, and architecture, which are judged for their aesthetics, or beauty. Fine art is sometimes discussed as being distinct from the applied arts, in which objects are equally valued for their beauty or design as well as for their usefulness or function, such as quilts or pottery.

flat: a) on a single plane; two-dimensional; or b) without variation or shading in color.

foreground: *see* background

fresco: technique of painting an image using pigment and water on a newly applied, still moist layer of lime plaster. The colors penetrate the plaster and are bound, or made permanent, by the lime.

gallery: a place where artwork is displayed, often for sale.

genre painting: paintings that portray scenes from everyday life.

geometric: of or pertaining to shapes from geometry such as circles, triangles, and squares.

gouache: a medium where the watercolor pigment has been mixed with a white gum preparation. When it is applied to the paper, this paint is opaque (the paper is not visible through the paint). Conversely, in watercolor painting, the paint is translucent, which means the paper is visible through the paint.

graphic artist: someone who makes drawings or prints.

hue: the tint or particular quality of a color, usually with reference to the primary hues (red, blue, and yellow) and colors that result from combinations of those three.

illustration: an image that is added to a text to give the reader additional insight into the author's ideas. Paintings, photographs, prints, or drawings are often used as illustrations for stories, poems, or articles in books or magazaines.

impressionism: a movement in painting whose aim was to reproduce the effects of light on the objects depicted. The impressionists applied small strokes of pure color that were intended to blend in the viewer's eye. The name comes from a painting by Claude Monet called *Impression: Sunrise* (1872). The movement had its origins in France in the 1860s, where it was initially met with scorn and suspicion. By the 1880s, impressionists were enjoying success and many American artists considered study in Paris essential. By the turn of the century it was a dominant influence in contemporary painting.

landscape/seascape: a painting or photograph that depicts a scene from nature.

Masonite: a type of fiberboard; some artists paint on Masonite.

medium (plural: mediums): a) in general, the material or process used by the artist. b) a category of art such as sculpture or photography.

mixed media: a work of art made up of various materials. The medium has its roots in sculpture.

modern art: a) any art produced in the present or recent past. b) art that questions or rejects traditional subjects or techniques. c) art from about the second half of the nineteenth century through World War I.

motif: a figure or shape that appears repeatedly in a work of art.

naïve: painting or sculpture produced in Western cultures that lacks or ignores some of the conventions of proportion or perspective that are part of Western art tradition.

neoclassicism: art from the late eighteenth through the early nineteenth centuries that pays tribute to the forms and ideals of ancient Greek and Roman art.

non-objective art: a term used to describe some kinds of abstract art that is completely separated from representing the appearance of the world around us. It is most often used to refer to severely geometric works.

palette: a) a piece of board, metal, or other material, usually with a hole for the thumb, on which an artist places and mixes paint. b) the range of colors an artist uses in a painting or body of work.

patron: a person who provides free and generous support to an artist; a patron often purchases or commissions works by an artist or promotes the artist's work with influential people or institutions.

photomontage: a) a strict category of collage that uses only pieces of photographs to create a new image. b) a work created by this process.

pigment: a substance that imparts color or black or white to other materials, especially a powdered substance mixed with a liquid to create inks or paints.

portrait: a work of art that depicts a person's likeness, and often carries clues about the person's qualities, profession, and standing in society.

primitivism: during the twentieth century it became common for some Western artists to seek out and use forms and imagery from some non-Western cultures, including Africa. Artists saw these forms and images as powerful and authentic.

print: artists make prints by etching, carving, or otherwise creating an image on stone, wood, metal, or another surface; covering the surface with ink; and then transferring the image onto a paper or cloth. Once the printing surface is prepared, the artist can make multiple copies of the print.

public art: art designed and created for a large place where the general public can easily see it, such as in a shopping mall, a park, or a train station; in a broader sense, art that is created to be situated in a specific community.

realism: the portrayal of people, places, and things as they appear in real life. Realism often carries the idea of accuracy and the concrete physical nature of the objects depicted, but can also suggest a rejection of the conventional or sentimental subjects in favor of nonidealized modern life.

regionalism: a movement in American painting that began during the 1930s and favored the rural over the urban. Its principal members—Thomas Hart Benton, John Stuart Curry, and Grant Wood—preferred to offer provincial scenes, particularly of the Midwest. Among their stated aims was a desire to create a uniquely American art that concentrated on local themes and rejected European influences.

representational art: art in which objects and figures are painted or sculpted as they appear to the eye; the opposite of abstract, or non-representational, art.

still-life painting: the portrayal of an arrangement of inanimate objects such as flowers, fruits, tools, or household items; still lifes often include reminders about time's swift passing and the certainty of death, or are a display of a painter's technical skill.

studio: the room where an artist works, usually furnished with the tools of the trade and materials used for inspiration.

study: a painting or drawing in which an artist works out various aspects of a composition. Some artists do many studies before beginning an important work.

tempera: a type of paint for which the pigments are ground in water and mixed with one of several mediums to form an emulsion. Egg white or egg yolk have been used for many centuries, and create a very stable paint that remains true in color even after hundreds of years.

textile artist: someone who creates works of art using cloth and fiber, sometimes in combination with paint or collage.

tint: a gradation of color from intense to pale; tints of color usually refer to the amount of white mixed with the pigment.

NOTES

EARLY STRIVINGS

Page 10 On Johnson's background. Jennifer Bryan and Robert Torchia. "The Mysterious Portraitist Joshua Johnson." *Archives of American Art Journal* 36, no. 2 (1996), pp. 2–7.

Page 11 "self-taught genius . . . give satisfaction." Joshua Johnson, ad in *Baltimore Intelligencer* (December 19, 1798), quoted in Romare Bearden and Harry Henderson, *A History of African-American Artists, From 1792 to the Present* (New York: Pantheon, 1993), p.8.

Page 12 Edmonia Lewis's birthplace. Various sources give different places. Among them: Ohio; Albany, New York; and Newark, New Jersey.

Page 15 "the man . . . friend to my people." Edmonia Lewis to Lydia Maria Child, letter reprinted in *Liberator,* February 19, 1864, p. 31, quoted in Bearden and Henderson, *A History*, p.60.

Page 19 "absolutely repellant." William J. Clark, Jr., *Great American Sculptures* (1878), quoted in Stephen May, "The Object at Hand," *Smithsonian* magazine, September 1996. Available at *www.smithsonianmag.si.edu*. **"the most remarkable . . . section."** J.S. Ingram, *The Centennial Exposition, Described and Illustrated* (1876), quoted in Stephen May, "The Object at Hand."

Page 22 "poems of peace." George W. Whitaker, "Reminiscences of Providence Artists," *Providence Magazine* (March 1914), quoted in Bearden and Henderson, *A History*, p. 48.

Page 22–23 On Bannister's confirmation of his win. Edward Bannister, quoted by George W. Whitaker, "Reminiscences," quoted in Hartigan, *Sharing Traditions*, p. 69–70. **"a couple of scraggy brushes."** Henry Tanner, "The Story of an Artist's Life," *World's Work*, vol. 18 (June-July 1909), quoted in Marcia M. Mathews, *Henry Ossawa Tanner: American Artist* (1969). Reprint (Chicago: University of Chicago Press, 1994), p. 13. **"Coming home . . . first effort."** Henry Tanner, "The Story of an Artist's Life," quoted in Mathews, *Henry Ossawa Tanner*, p. 14.

GREAT AWAKENINGS
Page 36 "African sculpture has . . . fresh motifs." Alain Locke, "The Legacy of the Ancestral Arts," in *The New Negro* (1925). Reprint, with an introduction by Arnold Rampersad (New York: Atheneum, 1992), p. 256. Locke's anthology was an expansion of a March 1925 *Survey Graphic* special issue: "Harlem, Mecca of the New Negro."

Page 39 "kneeling in a fetal position." Theresa Leininger-Miller, *New Negro Artists in Paris: African American Painters and Sculptors in the City of Light, 1922–1934*. (New Brunswick, NJ: Rutgers University Press, 2001), p. 175. **Augusta Savage's surname.** She was born Augusta Fells. Savage was the surname of her second husband, James. Robert Poston was her third husband. **"Negress Denied . . . School,"** *New York Times*, April 24, 1923, 8:2, quoted in Leininger-Miller, *New Negro Artists*, p.169.

Page 44 "If I can inspire . . . more than that" Augusta Savage, according to Ted Poston, *Metropolitan* (January 1935), quoted in Bearden and Henderson, *A History*, p. 176.

Page 45–46 Palmer Hayden's name. His parents named him Peyton Cole Hedgeman. His name change came about when he entered the army, as a result of a clerical error. **"Keep at it . . . famous artist."** Palmer Hayden's teacher, quoted in Bearden and Henderson, *A History*, p. 157. **"Young artist . . . commercial artist,"** Palmer Hayden, quoted in Bearden and Henderson, *A History*, p. 158. **"When he saw me . . . ended the interview."** Palmer Hayden, quoted in Bearden and Henderson, *A History*, p. 158.

Page 47–51 "Cubism . . . couldn't tell a story." Palmer Hayden, quoted in Richard J. Powell, *Rhapsodies in Black: Art of the Harlem Renaissance* (1997), quoted in Leininger-Miller, *New Negro Artists*, p. 86. **"There were times . . . sit down and draw."** Hale Woodruff, "Oral History Interview with Hale Woodruff" by Al Murray, November 18, 1968, Archives of American Art, Smithsonian Institution (*http://artarchives.si.edu/oralhist/woodru68.htm*). **"Come on . . . pass the summer."** Hale Woodruff, "Oral History Interview with Hale Woodruff."

Page 52 "These were the . . . congregated." Hale Woodruff, "Oral History Interview with Hale Woodruff." Interviewed by Al Murray, November 18, 1968, Archives of American Art, Smithsonian Institution.

Page 53–54 "Woodruff . . . African art." Hermann Lieber, quoted in "Oral History Interview with Hale Woodruff." **"You can't imagine . . . a real turning point for me."** Hale Woodruff, quoted in Bearden and Henderson, *A History*, p. 201. **"To tell you the truth . . . in the museums."** Hale Woodruff, quoted in Benny Andrews, "Hailing Hale Woodruff," *Encore American and Worldwide News*, April 3, 1978, p. 31, quoted in Leininger-Miller, *New Negro Artists*, p. 116. **"I had never seen such color before!"** Hale Woodruff, quoted in Leininger-Miller, *New Negro Artists*, p. 113. **"There's always . . . significance of the self."** Hale Woodruff, "Oral History Interview with Hale Woodruff."

Page 56 **"if any . . . destroyed."** John H. Hewitt, "Remembering Hale Woodruff," *International Review of African American Art*, vol. 13, no. 4, 1997 ("Fresh Paint"), p. 56.

Page 58 **"On the week . . . buried the feature forever."** Hale Woodruff, "Oral History Interview with Hale Woodruff."

Page 59 **"sensed in him . . . ability."** Charles Alston, quoted in Bearden and Henderson, *A History*, p. 261.

Page 63 **"The show . . . impression on me."** Jacob Lawrence, quoted in Bearden and Henderson, *A History*, p. 296.

Page 66 **"I am not afraid to . . . the canvas."** William H. Johnson, letter to Charles Hawthorne, Cagnes, France, quoted in unsigned, "Art and Life of William H. Johnson: A Guide for Teachers" (*www.americanart.si.edu*).

Page 69 **"He is a real . . . vigorous, firm and direct."** Harmon Foundation judges, statement, Exhibition of Fine Arts by American Negro Artists (1930), quoted in Bearden and Henderson, *A History*, p. 189.

Page 70 **"In all my years . . . existed."** William H. Johnson, quoted in Nora Holt, "Primitives on Exhibit," *New York Amsterdam News*, March 9, 1946, p. 16. Quoted in Richard J. Powell, *Homecoming: The Art and Life of William H. Johnson* (New York: Rizzoli, 1991), p. 213.

UPWARD & OUTWARD

Page 73 **"drew all the time . . . my mission."** Hughie Lee-Smith, quoted in Carol Wald, "The Metaphysical World of Hughie Lee-Smith," *American Artist,* vol. 43, October 1978, p. 53.

Page 74–76 **"In my case, aloneness, . . . much more in my youth."** Hughie Lee-Smith, quoted in Carol Wald, "The Metaphysical World of Hughie Lee-Smith," p. 101. **"All my things . . . razor's edge."** John Biggers, quoted in label copy to *Shotgun, Third Ward #1*, in the Smithsonian American Art Museum's exhibition Free Within Ourselves: African-American Art in the Collection of the National Museum of American Art, October 28, 1994–February 26, 1995.

Page 80 **"Charlie White had . . . my work,"** John Biggers, quoted in Mae Tate, "John Biggers: The Man and His Art," *International Review of African American Art*, vol. 7, no. 3, 1987 ("The Heartland"), p. 46. **"apprentice in an informal sense"** John Biggers, quoted in Mae Tate, "John Biggers: The Man and His Art," p. 46. **"We stood around . . . Harriet-the-Moses."** John Biggers, quoted in Bearden and Henderson, *A History*, p. 431.

Page 81 **"Perhaps I should . . . brush."** James Baldwin, quoted in Richard A. Long, *Beauford Delaney: A Retrospective* (New York: The Studio Museum in Harlem, exhibition catalogue, April 9–July 2, 1978), unpaginated.

Page 82 **"I had a magnificent . . . belonging"** John Biggers, "His Influence Caused Me to Turn Out Little Charles Whites," *Freedomways*, vol. 12., no. 3, 1980, quoted in H.E. Mahal, "Interviews: Four Afro-American Artists," *Art Gallery*, April 1970, p. 38.

Page 85 **"I paint . . . not collage."** Romare Bearden, "Oral History Interview with Romare Bearden" by Carol Fortress, June 28, 1970, Archives of American Art, Smithsonian Institution.

Page 86 **"He did marvelous . . . in all the rooms."** Romare Bearden, quoted in June Kelly, "Romare Bearden," *International Review of African American Art,* vol. 9, no. 4, 1991, ("Artists of the 30s and 40s"), p. 19. **Bearden's degree in education**. Based on confirming research by the curator of The Art of Romare Bearden, National Gallery of Art, September 14, 2003–January 4, 2004. References to Bearden having earned a degree in mathematics are in error.

Page 90 "the life . . . as I know it." Romare Bearden, quoted in Myron Schwartzman, *Romare Bearden: His Life and Art* (New York: Harry N. Abrams, 1990), p. 204.

Page 92 "Through the camera . . . directly." Roy DeCarava, *Photographs,* ed. James Albinder, introduction by Sherry Turner DeCarava (Carmel, Calif.: The Friends of Photography, 1981), p. 8

Page 95 "So I had . . . no place to show them." Roy DeCarava, quoted in David Vestal, "In the Key of Life," *Camera Arts,* May 1983, p. 87. **"But after that . . . quiet."** Roy DeCarava, quoted in David Vestal, "In the Key of Life," p. 87. **"a familiar presence"** Roy DeCarava, quoted in "Milieu: The Harlem Community Art Center and the WPA" in *Creative Space: Fifty Years of Robert Blackburn's Printmaking Workshop.* Library of Congress. *www.loc.gov/exhibbits/blackburn/* **"Why don't you do a book?"** Langston Hughes, quoted in David Vestal, "In the Key of Life," p. 88.

Page 96–97 "because it signified . . . the national stage." Louis H. Draper, Abstract to Photography Institute lecture "Kamoinge: The Members, the Cohesion and Evolution of the Group" June 12, 1995 (*www.thephotographyinstitute.org/www/all_abstracts/1995.html*). **"I remember . . . fowl."** Alma Thomas, quoted in Eleanor C. Munro, "Alma W. Thomas" in *Originals: American Women Artists* (New York: Simon & Schuster, 1979), p. 191. **"put on their display for us."** Alma Thomas, quoted in Eleanor C. Munro, "Alma W. Thomas," p. 191. **"most unusual wildflowers."** Alma Thomas, quoted in Eleanor C. Munro, "Alma W. Thomas," p. 191. **"Color is . . . light."** Johannes Itten, *The Art of Color: The Subjective Experience and Objective Rationale of Color,* trans. Ernst van Haagen (New York: Reinhold, 1961), p. 13.

Page 98–99 "When I entered . . . heaven." Alma Thomas, quoted in Eleanor C. Munro, "Alma W. Thomas," p. 193. **"This is the end . . . walk."** Alma Thomas, quoted in Eleanor C. Munro, "Alma W. Thomas," p. 194. **"When I was . . . times have changed."** Alma Thomas, quoted in David L. Shirey, "At 77, She's Made It to the Whitney," *New York Times,* May 4, 1972, p. 52. **"Time to wake up . . . our souls."** Sister Gertrude Morgan, quoted in Rosemary Kent, "Sister Gertrude," Interview, *The States-Item* (New Orleans) September 1, 1973.

Page 103–104 "[The Throne] may well be . . . an American," Robert Hughes, "Overdressing for the Occasion," *Time* (April 5, 1976), **"I turned and . . . into dazzling altars of gold and silver."** Betye Saar, "Temple for Tomorrow," *American Art,* summer/fall 1994, p. 130. **"I'd go out in . . . the dirt."** Betye Saar, quoted in Eleanor C. Munro, "Betye Saar," p. 356. **"A curiosity about the mystical,"** Betye Saar, artist's statement (*www.bisaar.com*).

Page 106 "looking . . . into myself," Renée Stout, quoted in Wyatt MacGaffey and Michael D. Harris, *Astonishment and Power* (Washington, D.C.: Smithsonian Institution Press/National Museum of African Art, 1993), p. 121.

Page 108 "create art . . . about their own existence." Renée Stout, artist's statement accompanying exhibition Dear Robert, I'll Meet You at the Crossroads: A Project by Renée Stout, at the Bronx Museum of Art (1995), quoted in Lynda Roscoe Hartigan, "Spiritual Expressions," in Jacquelyn Days Serwer, ed., *American Kaleidoscope: Themes and Perspectives in Recent Art* (Washington, D.C.: Distributed Art Publishers/National Museum of American Art, 1996), p. 52.

Page 110 "African Americans . . . to the history of world ceramics." Winnie Owens-Hart, "Traditions: Ipetumodu," *International Review of African American Art,* vol. 11, no. 2, 1994 ("Toward Definition: An Examination of African American Craft Art"), p. 59. **"The making of . . . civilizations."** Winnie Owens-Hart, artist's statement for April 11–June 1, 1997 exhibition at Hand Workshop Art Center in Richmond, Virginia.

Page 112 "fantasized . . . life." Faith Ringgold, *We Flew Over the Bridge: The Memoirs of Faith Ringgold* (Boston: Bulfinch Press, Little, Brown and Co.,1995), p. 254.

SELECTED BIBLIOGRAPHY

Bearden, Romare and Harry Henderson. *A History of African-American Artists, From 1792 to the Present*. New York: Pantheon, 1993.

Campbell, Mary Schmidt, et al. *Harlem Renaissance: Art of Black America*. New York: Harry N. Abrams/The Studio Museum in Harlem, 1987.

DeCarava, Roy and Langston Hughes. *The Sweet Flypaper of Life* (1955). Reprint. Washington, D.C.: Howard University Press, 1984.

Everett, Gwen. *African American Masters: Highlights from the Smithsonian American Art Museum*. New York: Harry N. Abrams/Smithsonian American Art Museum, 2003.

Fine, Ruth, et al. *The Art of Romare Bearden*. New York: Harry N. Abrams, 2003.

Galassi, Peter. *Roy DeCarava: A Retrospective*. New York: Museum of Modern Art, 1996.

Gips, Terry, et al. *Narratives of African American Identity: The David C. Driskell Collection*. San Francisco: Pomegranate, 1998.

Greene, Carroll, interviewer. "Oral History Interview with Jacob Lawrence," 26 October 1968, Smithsonian Archives of American Art: *http://artarchives.si.edu/oralhist/lawren68.htm*.

Hartigan, Lynda Roscoe. "James Hampton's *Throne*," catalogue for exhibition at Montgomery Museum of Fine Arts, 8 March-8 June 1977.

———. *Sharing Traditions: Five Black Artists in Nineteenth-Century America*. Washington, D.C.: Smithsonian Institution Press/National Museum of American Art, 1985.

Hewitt, John H. "Remembering Hale A. Woodruff," *International Review of African American Art*, vol. 13, no. 4, 1997 ("Fresh Paint"): pp. 51-6.

Hewitt, M.J. "Betye Saar, An Interview," *International Review of African American Art,* vol. 10, no. 2, 1992: ("The Spirit of Ritual, The Magic of Technology: Performance, Installation and Digital Art."): pp. 6–23.

Leininger-Miller, Theresa. *New Negro Artists in Paris: African American Painters and Sculptors in the City of Light, 1922–1934*. New Brunswick, N.J.: Rutgers University Press, 2001.

Lewis, Samella. *African-American Art and Artists*. Berkeley and Los Angeles: University of California Press, 1990.

——— ed. *International Review of African American Art*, vol. 9, no. 4, 1991: "Artists of the 30s and 40s."

——— ed. *International Review of African American Art*, vol. 11, no. 3, 1994: "Image and Identity: The African American Experience in 20th Century American Art."

——— ed. *International Review of African American Art*, vol. 12, no. 4, 1995: "Institutional Murals."

Livingstone, Jane and John Beardsley, with a contribution by Regenia Perry. *Black Folk Art in America, 1930–1980*. Jackson, Miss.: University Press of Mississippi/Corcoran Gallery of Art, 1982.

Locke, Alain. *The New Negro* (1925). Reprint, with an introduction by Arnold Rampersad. New York: Atheneum, 1992.

MacGaffey, Wyatt and Michael D. Harris. *Astonishment and Power* (containing "The Eyes of Understanding: Kongo Minkisi" by MacGaffey, and "The Art of Renee Stout" by Harris). Washington, D.C.: Smithsonian Institution Press, 1993.

Mathews, Marcia M. *Henry Ossawa Tanner: American Artist*. Chicago: University of Chicago Press, 1995.

Mosby, Dewey F., et al. *Henry Ossawa Tanner*. New York: Rizzoli/Philadelphia Museum of Art, 1991.

Munro, Eleanor C. "Alma W. Thomas" and "Betye Saar" in *Originals: American Women Artists* (pp: 189–97; 355–61). New York: Simon & Schuster, 1979.

Murray, Al, interviewer. "Oral History Interview with Hale Woodruff," 18 November 1968, Smithsonian Archives of American Art: *http://artarchives.si.edu/oralhist/woodru68.htm*.

Nesbett, Peter T. and Michelle DuBois, eds. *Over the Line: The Art and Life of Jacob Lawrence*. Seattle: University of Washington Press, 2000.

———. *Jacob Lawrence: Paintings, Drawings, and Murals (1935–1999): A Catalogue Raisonné*. Seattle: University of Washington Press, 2000.

Owens-Hart, Winnie. "Traditions: Ipetumodu," *International Review of African American Art* vol. 11, no. 2, 1994 ("Toward Definition: An Examination of African American Craft Art"), pp. 59–60

Patton, Sharon F. *African-American Art*. New York: Oxford University Press, 1998.

Perry, Regenia, et al. *Free Within Ourselves: African-American Artists in the Collection of the National Museum of American Art*. San Francisco: Pomegranate, 1999.

Porter, James A. *Modern Negro Art* (1943). Reprint with a new introduction by David C. Driskell. Washington, D.C.: Howard University Press, 1992.

Powell, Richard. *Homecoming: The Art and Life of William H. Johnson*. New York: Rizzoli, 1991.

Schwartzman, Myron. *Romare Bearden: His Life and Art*. New York: Harry N. Abrams, 1990.

Turner, Elizabeth Hutton, ed. *Jacob Lawrence: The Migration Series*. Washington, D.C.: Rappahannock Press, 1993.

Wald, Carol. "The Metaphysical World of Hughie Lee-Smith," *American Artists*, October 1978, pp. 48–53, 101, 102.

Wardlaw, Alvia J., with essays by Edmund Barry Gaither, et al. *The Art of John Biggers: View from the Upper Room*. New York: Harry N. Abrams/The Museum of Fine Arts, Houston, 1995.

———, et al, eds. *Black Art Ancestral Legacy: The African Impulse in African-American Art*. New York: Harry N. Abrams/Dallas Museum of Art, 1989.

Wheat, Ellen Harkins, with a contribution by Patricia Hills. *Jacob Lawrence: American Painter*. Seattle: University of Washington Press/Seattle Art Museum, 1986.

Willis, Deborah. *Reflections in Black: A History of Black Photographers, 1840 to the Present*. New York: W. W. Norton, 2000.

Willis-Braithwaite, Deborah and Rodger C. Birt. *VanDerZee: Photographer, 1886–1983*. New York: Harry N. Abrams/National Portrait Gallery, Smithsonian Institution, 1998.

SUGGESTED READING

Butler, Jerry. *A Drawing in the Sand: A Story of African American Art*. Madison, Wis.: Zino Press Children's Books, 1999.

Duggleby, John. *Story Painter: The Life of Jacob Lawrence*. San Francisco: Chronicle Books, 1998.

Everett, Gwen. *Li'L Sis and Uncle Willie: A Story Based on the Life and Paintings of William H. Johnson*. New York: Rizzoli/National Musuem of American Art, 1991.

Finley, Carol. *The Art of African Masks: Exploring Cultural Traditions*. Minneapolis, Minn.: Lerner Publications, 1999.

Greenberg, Jan, ed. *Romare Bearden: Collage of Memories*. New York: Harry N. Abrams, 2003.

———, ed. *Heart to Heart: New Poems Inspired by Twentieth Century American Art*. New York: Harry N. Abrams, 2001.

Haskins, Jim. *Black Stars of the Harlem Renaissance*. New York: John Wiley & Sons, 2002.

Janson, W. H. and Anthony F. Janson. *A History of Art for Young People*. New York: Abrams Books for Young Readers, 1997.

Johnson, Dinah. *All Around Town: The Photographs of Richard Samuel Roberts*. New York: Henry Holt, 1998.

Johnson, James Weldon, illustrated by Elizabeth Catlett. *Lift Every Voice and Sing*. New York: Walker & Co., 1993.

Knapp, Ruthie and Janice Lehmberg. *Off the Wall Museum Guides for Kids*. The series includes "French Impressionist Art" (1998), "Greek and Roman Art" (2001), and "Modern Art" (2001). Worcester, MA: Davis Publications.

Lawrence, Jacob, with a poem of appreciation by Walter Dean Myers. *The Great Migration: An American Story*. New York: HarperCollins/ The Museum of Modern Art/The Phillips Collection, 1993.

Leach, Deba Foxley. *I See You, I See Myself: The Young Life of Jacob Lawrence*. Washington, D.C.: Phillips Collection, 2002.

Lyons, Mary. *Deep Blues: Bill Traylor, Self-Taught Artist*. New York: Atheneum, 1995.

———. *Starting Home: The Story of Horace Pippin, Painter*. New York: Scribner's, 1993.

———. *Stitching Stars: The Story Quilts of Harriet Powers*. New York: Scribner's, 1993; Alladin, 1997.

———*Talking With Tebé: Clementine Hunter, Memory Artist*. Boston: Houghton, Mifflin, 1998.

Ringgold, Faith, et al. *Talking to Faith Ringgold*. New York: Crown, 1996.

Rochelle, Belinda, ed. *Words with Wings: A Treasury of African-American Poetry and Art*. New York: HarperCollins/Amistad, 2001.

Sullivan, Charles, ed. *Children of Promise: African American Literature and Art for Young People*. New York: Harry N. Abrams, 1991.

ILLUSTRATION CREDITS

Cover *The Library* (detail), 1960, by Jacob Lawrence. Tempera on fiberboard, 24 x 29 7/8 in. Smithsonian American Art Museum, Gift of S. C. Johnson & Son, Inc. Frontispiece *Afro Emblems* (detail), 1950, by Hale Woodruff. Oil on linen, 18 x 22 in. Smithsonian American Art Museum, Gift of Mr. and Mrs. Alfred T. Morris, Jr. Page 6 *Still Life with Peonies*, 1949, by James Porter. Oil on canvas, 40 x 30 1/8 in. Smithsonian American Art Museum, Museum purchase through the Luisita L. and Franz H. Denghausen Endowment and the Smithsonian Institution Collections Acquisition Program; James A. Porter, photographed by Milan Uzelac. Courtesy of Coni Porter Uzelac Page 8 *Oak Trees* (detail), 1876, by Edward Mitchell Bannister. Oil on canvas, 33 7/8 x 60 1/4 in. Smithsonian American Art Museum, Gift of H. Alan and Melvin Frank Page 10 Bill of sale and manumission for Joshua Johnson, recorded in 1782, Maryland Historical Society, Baltimore Page 11 *Portrait of Adelia Ellender*,

about 1830–1832, by Joshua Johnson. Oil on canvas, 26 1/4 x 21 1/8 in. Smithsonian American Art Museum, Gift of Mr. and Mrs. Norman Robbins Page 12 Edmonia Lewis, about 1870, photographed by Henry Rocher. Albumen silver print, Image/sheet: 3 5/8 x 2 1/16 in. National Portrait Gallery, Smithsonian Institution Page 14 *Moses (after Michelangelo)*, 1875, by Edmonia Lewis. Marble, 26 3/4 x 11 1/2 x 13 5/8 in. Smithsonian American Art Museum, Gift of Mr. and Mrs. Alfred T. Morris, Jr. Page 17 *Old Arrow Maker*, modeled 1866, carved 1872, by Edmonia Lewis. Marble, 21 1/2 x 13 5/8 x 13 3/8 in. Smithsonian American Art Museum, Gift of Mr. and Mrs. Norman Robbins Page 18 *The Death of Cleopatra*, carved 1876, by Edmonia Lewis. Marble, 63 x 31 1/4 x 46 in. Smithsonian American Art Museum, Gift of the Historical Society of Forest Park, Illinois Page 19 Edward Mitchell Bannister, about 1875, photographed by Gustine L. Hurd. Albumen silver print, Image:

5 11/16 x 4 in. National Portrait Gallery, Smithsonian Institution, Gift of Sandra and Jacob Terner Pages 20–21 *Oak Trees*, 1876, by Edward Mitchell Bannister. Oil on canvas, 33 7/8 x 60 1/4 in. Smithsonian American Art Museum, Gift of H. Alan and Melvin Frank Page 23 Henry O. Tanner at work, about 1935, by unknown photographer. Henry Ossawa Tanner papers, 1850–1978 (bulk 1890–1920), Archives of American Art, Smithsonian Institution Page 24 *Abraham's Oak*, 1905, by Henry Ossawa Tanner. Oil on canvas, 21 3/8 x 28 5/8 in. Smithsonian American Art Museum, Gift of Mr. and Mrs. Norman Robbins Page 26 *The Banjo Lesson*, 1893, by Henry Ossawa Tanner. Oil on canvas, 49 x 35 1/2 in. Hampton University Museum, Hampton, Virginia Page 28 *Study for the Raising of Lazarus*, by Henry Ossawa Tanner. Oil on plywood, 6 x 7 7/8 in. Smithsonian American Art Museum, Gift of Mr. and Mrs. Norman Robbins Page 30 Robert Scott Duncanson, about 1863–1865,

photographed by N. J. Mitchell. Private collection, Canada Page 31 *Vulture and Its Prey*, 1844, by Robert Scott Duncanson. Oil on canvas, 27 1/8 x 22 1/4 in. Smithsonian American Art Museum, Gift of Harold E. Deal Page 32 *I Baptize Thee* (detail), about 1940, by William H. Johnson. Oil on burlap, 38 1/8 x 45 1/2 in. Smithsonian American Art Museum, Gift of the Harmon Foundation Page 34 (left) *Self-Portrait*, 1934, by Malvin Gray Johnson. Oil on canvas, 38 1/4 x 30 in. Smithsonian American Art Museum, Gift of the Harmon Foundation; (right) Malvin Gray Johnson, by unknown photographer. Courtesy of National Archives Page 37 (left) James VanDerZee, 1982, photographed by Kurt Edward Fishback, © Kurt Edward Fishback; (right) *Evening Attire*, 1922, by James VanDerZee. Gelatin silver print, 10 x 8 in. Smithsonian American Art Museum, Museum Purchase through the Julia D. Strong Endowment and the Smithsonian Institution Collections Acquisition Program Page 38 Augusta Savage with her sculpture *Realization*, about 1938, photographed by Herman for the Works Progress Administration. Photographs of Artists—Microfilm Collection I, Archives of American Art, Smithsonian Institution. Page 40 *Gamin*, about 1929, by Augusta Savage. Painted plaster, 9 x 5 3/4 x 4 3/8 in. Smithsonian American Art Museum, Gift of Benjamin and Olya Margolin Page 43 *Lift Every Voice and Sing*, 1939, by Augusta Savage. Painted plaster, 16 ft. high. Photograph by Carl Van Vechten, Van Vechten Trust, 1939, Yale Collection of American Literature, Beinecke Rare Book and Manuscript Library Page 45 Palmer Hayden returning from Paris, 1932, by unknown photographer. Palmer C. Hayden papers, 1924–1967, Archives of American Art, Smithsonian Institution Page 46 *The Janitor Who Paints*, about 1937, by Palmer Hayden. Oil on canvas, 39 1/8 x 32 7/8 in. Smithsonian American Art Museum, Gift of the Harmon Foundation Pages 48–49 *John Henry on the Right, Steam Drill on the Left*, 1944–1947, by Palmer Hayden. Oil on canvas, 30 x 40 in. Museum of African American Art, Los Angeles Page 50 *Midnight at the Crossroads*, about 1940, by Palmer Hayden. Oil on canvas, 28 x 34 in. © Miriam Hayden Estate, Courtesy M. Hanks Gallery, Santa Monica, California, Collection Robert and Faye Davidson Page 52 *Georgia Landscape*, about 1934–1935, by Hale Woodruff. Oil on canvas, 21 1/8 x 25 5/8 in. Smithsonian American Art Museum, Gift of Mr. and Mrs. Alfred T. Morris, Jr. Page 53 Portrait of Hale Woodruff, 1966, photogra-phed by Henry Clements. First World Festival of Negro Arts photographs/[Geoffrey Clements], Archives of American Art, Smithsonian Institution. Page 55 *Afro Emblems*, 1950, by Hale Woodruff. Oil on linen, 18 x 22 in. Smithsonian American Art Museum, Gift of Mr. and Mrs. Alfred T. Morris, Jr. Page 56 *Back to Africa* from "The Amistad Murals," 1938–1939, by Hale Woodruff. Oil on canvas, 42 x 78 in. Talladega College, Alabama Page 59 Portrait of Jacob Lawrence, California, 1957 by Alfredo Valente. Alfredo Valente papers, 1941–1978, Archives of American Art, Smithsonian Institution. Pages 60–61 *And the Migrants Kept Coming*, Panel 60 from "The Migration Series," 1940–1941 (text and title revised by the artist, 1993), by Jacob Lawrence. Tempera on gesso on composition board, 12 x 18 in. The Museum of Modern Art, New York. Gift of Ms. David M. Levy. Digital Image © 2003 The Museum of Modern Art, New York

Page 62 *Captain Skinner*, 1944, by Jacob Lawrence. Gouache on paperboard, 29 1/8 x 21 1/8 in. Smithsonian American Art Museum, Gift of Carlton Skinner Page 64 *The Library*, 1960, by Jacob Lawrence. Tempera on fiberboard, 24 x 29 7/8 in. Smithsonian American Art Museum, Gift of S. C. Johnson & Son, Inc. Page 66 William H. Johnson, painting, by unknown photographer. Courtesy of National Archives Page 67 *Fruit Trees and Mountains*, about 1936–1938, by William H. Johnson. Oil on burlap, 28 1/2 x 35 1/8 in. Smithsonian American Art Museum, Gift of the Harmon Foundation Page 68 *Children at Ice Cream Stand*, about 1939–1942, by William H. Johnson. Tempera, pen and ink, and pencil on paper, 12 5/8 x 15 in. Smithsonian American Art Museum, Gift of the Harmon Foundation Page 70 *I Baptize Thee*, about 1940, by William H. Johnson. Oil on burlap, 38 1/8 x 45 1/2 in. Smithsonian American Art Museum, Gift of the Harmon Foundation Page 72 *Jesus Is My Air Plane* (detail), about 1970, by Sister Gertrude Morgan. Tempera, ballpoint pen and ink, and pencil on paper, 18 x 26 3/8 in. Smithsonian American Art Museum, Gift of Herbert Waide Hemphill, Jr. and museum purchase made possible by Ralph Cross Johnson Page 74 Hughie Lee-Smith, 1993, photographed by Patricia Lee-Smith. Courtesy of June Kelly Gallery, New York Page 75 *The Stranger*, about 1957–1958, by Hughie Lee-Smith. Oil on canvas, 26 1/4 x 36 1/8 in. Smithsonian American Art Museum, Museum purchase Page 76 John Biggers at home, 1997 photographed by Nancy Walkup Page 77 (left) Lois Mailou Jones, by unknown photographer. Courtesy of National Archives; (right) *Les Fétiches*, 1938, by Lois Mailou Jones. Oil on linen, 21 x 25 1/2 in. Smithsonian American Art Museum, Museum purchase made possible by Mrs. N. H. Green, Dr. R. Harlan, and Francis Musgrave Pages 78–79 *Shotgun, Third Ward #1*, 1966, by John Biggers. Tempera and oil on canvas, 30 x 48 in. Smithsonian American Art Museum, Museum purchase made possible by Anacostia Museum, Smithsonian Institution Page 81 (left) Beauford Delaney, about 1970, photographed by Emil Cadoo. Gelatin Silver print. Courtesy of Michael Rosenfeld Gallery, LLC, New York, and Janos Gat Gallery, New York; (right) *Abstraction*, by Beauford Delaney. Gouache on paper, 22 1/2 x 17 in. Smithsonian American Art Museum, Gift of Maurice and Margery Katz Page 83 (left) Joseph Delaney, photographed by Fern Logan, © Fern Logan; (right) *Penn Station at War Time*, 1943, by Joseph Delaney. Oil on canvas, 34 x 48 1/8 in. Smithsonian American Art Museum, Gift of Joseph Delaney Page 84 Romare Bearden, 1980, photographed by Hans Namuth. Cibachrome on paper, Image: 19 15/16 x 13 9/16 in.; Sheet: 19 15/16 x 15 7/8 in. National Portrait Gallery, Smithsonian Institution; this acquisition was made possible by a generous contribution from the James Smithson Society Page 85 *Spring Way*, 1964, by Romare Bearden. Collage on paperboard, 6 5/8 x 9 3/8 in. Smithsonian American Art Museum, Bequest of Henry Ward Ranger through the National Academy of Design Page 87 (left) Norman Lewis (detail), photographed by Juley Studio. Peter A. Juley & Son Collection, Smithsonian American Art Museum; (right) *Evening Rendezvous*, 1962, by Norman Lewis. Oil on linen, 50 1/4 x 64 1/4 in. Smithsonian American Art Museum, Museum purchase Pages 88–89 *Empress of

the Blues*, 1974, by Romare Bearden. Acrylic and pencil and printed paper on paperboard, 36 x 48 in. Smithsonian American Art Museum, Museum purchase in part through the Luisita L. and Franz H. Denghausen Endowment Page 91 (left) Felrath Hines (detail), photographed by Juley Studio. Peter A. Juley & Son Collection, Smithsonian American Art Museum; (right) *Yellow and Gray*, 1976, by Felrath Hines. Oil on linen, 54 1/4 x 48 in. Smithsonian American Art Museum, Gift of the Barbara Fiedler Gallery Page 92 Roy DeCarava, 1982, photographed by Kurt Edward Fishback. © Kurt Edward Fishback Page 93 *Graduation, New York*, 1949 (printed 1982), by Roy DeCarava. Gelatin silver print, 10 7/8 x 14 in. Smithsonian American Art Museum, Museum purchase made possible by Henry L. Milmore Page 94 (left) *Fort Scott, Kansas*, 1950, by Gordon Parks. Gelatin silver print, 13 1/2 x 9 1/2 in. Smithsonian American Art Museum, Museum purchase through the Horace W. Goldsmith Foundation; (right) Gordon Parks, 1945, photographed by Arnold Eagle. Gelatin silver print. Image: 9 5/8 x 7 15/16 in.; Sheet: 9 15/16 x 7 15/16 in. National Portrait Gallery, Smithsonian Institution. Page 96 Alma Thomas, about 1970, unknown photographer. Alma Thomas papers, 1894–1979, Archives of American Art, Smithsonian Institution Page 97 *Red Sunset, Old Pond Concerto*, 1972, by Alma Thomas. Acrylic on canvas, 68 1/2 x 52 1/4 in. Smithsonian American Art Museum, Gift of the Woodward Foundation Page 99 Sister Gertrude Morgan at New Orleans Jazz Festival, 1972, from a photograph by Michael P. Smith. © Michael P. Smith Pages 100–101 *Jesus Is My Air Plane*, about 1970, by Sister Gertrude Morgan. Tempera, ballpoint pen and ink, and pencil on paper, 18 x 26 3/8 in. Smithsonian American Art Museum, Gift of Herbert Waide Hemphill, Jr. and museum purchase made possible by Ralph Cross Johnson Page 102 *The Throne of the Third Heaven of the Nations' Millennium General Assembly*, about 1950–1964, by James Hampton. Gold and silver aluminum foil, Kraft paper, and plastic over wood furniture, paperboard, and glass (180 pieces in overall configuration), 10 1/2 x 27 x 14 1/2 ft. Smithsonian American Art Museum, Gift of anonymous donors Page 103 Photograph of James Hampton in his garage with *The Throne of the Third Heaven of the Nations' Millennium General Assembly*, by an unknown photographer. Smithsonian American Art Museum Page 104 Betye Saar photographed by Jimi Giannatti. © Jimi Giannatti; Courtesy of Michael Rosenfeld Gallery, LLC, New York, New York Page 105 *Wishing for Winter*, 1989, by Betye Saar. Mixed media, 40 3/4 x 19 1/4 x 2 1/4 in. Smithsonian American Art Museum, Museum purchase Page 106 Renée Stout, photographed by Greg Staley. Courtesy of the artist Page 107 *The Colonel's Cabinet*, 1991–1994, by Renée Stout. Mixed media: carpet, chair, painting, and cabinet with found and handmade objects, 67 1/2 x 60 x 50 1/2 in. Smithsonian American Art Museum, Museum purchase made possible by Ralph Cross Johnson Page 108 Winnie Owens-Hart, photographed by Jarvis Grant. Courtesy of the artist Page 109 *Drum with Reptile Motif*, 1993, by Winnie Owens-Hart. Fired earthenware, 10 x 11 x 10 in. Smithsonian American Art Museum, Museum purchase through the Renwick Acquisitions Fund Page 111 (left) Earlie Hudnall Jr., by unknown photographer. Courtesy of the artist; (right) *Lady in

Black Hat with Feathers, 1990, by Earlie Hudnall Jr. Gelatin silver print, 19 7/8 x 16 in. Smithsonian American Art Museum, Gift of the artist Page 112 Faith Ringgold photographic portrait, 1993, photographed by Grace Matthews. Grace Matthews © 1993 Page 113 *The Bitter Nest, Part II: The Harlem*

Renaissance Party, 1988, by Faith Ringgold. Acrylic on canvas with printed, dyed, and pieced fabric, 94 x 83 in. Smithsonian American Art Museum, Museum purchase Page 114 (left) Melvin Edwards, by unknown photographer. Courtesy of CDS Gallery, New York; (right) *Tambo,* 1993, by Melvin Edwards. Welded steel,

28 1/8 x 25 1/4 x 22 in. Smithsonian American Art Museum, Museum purchase through the Luisita L. and Franz H. Denghausen Endowment and the Smithsonian Institution Collections Acquisition Program

INDEX